The Threads of Public Policy:
A Study in Policy Leadership

The Urban Governors Series

The Threads
of Public Policy:
A Study
in Policy Leadership

Robert Eyestone
University of Minnesota

The Bobbs-Merrill Company, Inc.   Indianapolis   New York

Heinz Eulau, Stanford University
Kenneth Prewitt, University of Chicago

Coeditors, The Urban Governors Series

Editors' Preface

This study, like the others in *The Urban Governors* series, is based on data collected by the City Council Research Project, Institute of Political Studies, Stanford University. The CCRP was a collaborative research and research-training program made possible by grants from the National Science Foundation. Members of the project, all at one time or another doctoral candidates in political science at Stanford, were Betty H. Zisk, Boston University; Ronald O. Loveridge, University of California; Robert Eyestone, University of Minnesota; Peter A. Lupsha, Yale University; Thomas E. Cronin, University of North Carolina; Gordon Black, University of Rochester; Katherine Hinckley, Rice University; Stephen Ziony, City University of New York; Charles F. Levine, University of Illinois at Chicago Circle; and Helmut Kramer, Institute for Advanced Studies, Vienna. The editors served as principal and associate investigators, respectively.

Although CCRP was centrally directed, each investigator contributed to the design of the research and was free to utilize the commonly collected data as he saw fit. Each monograph in this series therefore reflects the writer's own theoretical and substantive interests, and each writer is alone responsible for what he has written. Yet, the series as a whole is more than the sum of its parts. At the heart of the project was a concern with decision-making in small, natural-state legislative groups. Decisions coming out of city councils have far-reaching consequences for the lives of residents in a metropolitan region. While the project's central focus was on legislative behavior within the city council, topics as diverse as problems of metropolitan integration or the socialization and recruitment experiences of individual councilmen became matters of inquiry. As a result, the individual monographs in this series are variously linked not only to the literature on legislatures and representation, but also to the literature on urban government, policy outputs, elections, interest group politics, and other aspects of political life.

The "web of government" is complex, and its complexity makes for complex analysis. We solved the problem of complexity in the real world of politics by dividing the analytic labor among the project's members, and this is the reason that each volume in this series must stand on its own feet. But we would also insist that each volume contribute to the common enterprise of managing the complexity of political life without imposing on it any fashionably simple model of what politics is all about. In general, the units of analysis used in the different monographs are individual councilmen. A comprehensive study based on councils rather than on councilmen as units of analysis is also in preparation.

The major source of data was interviews conducted with 435 city councilmen in eighty-seven cities of the greater San Francisco Bay region during 1966 and 1967. A description of the research site, research design, interview success, and related matters can be found in Appendix E. Some of the interviews were conducted by the members of the research team, but the bulk were undertaken by a group of professional interviewers including Jean J. Andrews, Sheryl Brown, Marion N. Fay, Helen M. Smelser, Sofia K. Thornburg, Mary E. Warren, and Betty E. Urquhart. Peter Lupsha served as field coordinator, Jean Stanislaw as research aid, and Virginia Anderson as project secretary. During the analytical phase of the project we have had the help of Sally Ferejohn as research assistant, Tex Hull as computer adviser, and Lois Renner as secretary.

Heinz Eulau
Kenneth Prewitt

CONTENTS

APPENDIXES

TABLES

FIGURES AND MAPS

Part I

The Councilmen and Their Cities

In recent years critics of the urban scene have questioned the ability of city governments to deal successfully with metropolitanism and its attendant problems. These observers decry what they see as urban sprawl, haphazard commercial and industrial development, inefficient duplication of services, overburdened tax arrangements, and inadequate service levels.[1] Metropolitan growth, they suggest, is still largely determined by social and economic forces far more powerful than the city governments that might try to control or to change these conditions. In the critics' view, the form that the political process takes in metropolitan areas discourages both the confrontation of important urban problems and the assembling of power sufficient to cope with them.[2] Whenever city governments have acted, they have simply implemented the inevitable.

The amount of money spent indicates that American cities obviously are trying to improve the urban environment. In addition to providing such basic services as police and fire protection, city governments today regularly sponsor park and recreation pro-

---

[1]See, for example, *Modernizing Local Government* (New York: Committee for Economic Development, 1966), and James A. Maxwell, *Financing State and Local Governments* (Washington, D.C.: The Brookings Institution, 1965). [2]See, for example, Raymond Vernon, *Metropolis 1985* (Cambridge, Mass.: Harvard University Press, 1960), Chapter 10, and Robert C. Wood, "The Contributions of Political Science to Urban Form," in Werner Z. Hirsch, ed., *Urban Life and Form* (New York: Holt, Rinehart & Winston, 1963), pp. 99–127.

grams, maintain library facilities, and underwrite beautification campaigns and other civic-minded projects. Welfare and health programs have a shorter history as ongoing responsibilities for city governments, but these programs too are now appearing in many cities as local politicians begin to recognize the need for them.

Critics who argue that efforts of this kind are insufficient frequently overlook the desires of city residents and the limited possibilities open to city decision-makers. These observers apply externally derived standards to the level of services provided rather than determining what the city's residents and leaders themselves want. In fact, the desires of residents are a more appropriate criterion for judging the performance of city governments than some hypothetically "necessary" level of services. Few cities will provide more than their citizens want, because each proposed service increase translates directly into higher taxes on property owners—whose collective voice leaders generally heed. On the other hand, political leaders acting in a favorable climate of opinion may contract for more services than the residents "need" according to some objective criterion.

This study differs from much existing research on city politics by taking policy leadership as its explicit focus. This approach assumes that the phenomenon of policy leadership is a more promising subject for research than abstract standards of service adequacy. Briefly, policy leadership is a special form of political leadership that may be exerted in a problematic situation. The policy leader is concerned with finding the appropriate course of action to deal with the problem in order to reach certain desired goals. As a concept, policy leadership is explicitly action-oriented and purposive, excluding the affective, symbolic, and solidary characteristics that the concept of political leadership implies.

Policy leadership cannot be exercised unless would-be policy leaders are faced with a problem, but the existence of a problem does not guarantee that policy leadership will occur. Most cities in a metropolitan region experience problems because they are in a rapidly growing area, but not all city governments attempt to deal with these problems in a systematic and purposeful man-

ner. Part of the difference between cities faced with similar problems may be the extent of policy leadership exercised by the
various city councils. Some city governments may recognize the
existence of problems and react to them, others may see the problems but be powerless to deal with them, while still others may
not perceive a problem until it is too late to act. These differences are the subject matter of this study.

Sweeping criticisms of the urban political process often ob-
scure important variations from city to city. By arguing that
urban politics in general is unable to cope with metropolitan
problems, critics beg the question of the adequacy of the policy
process in individual cities. It is difficult to determine, for instance, how much freedom city councils have in choosing policies
for their cities and how much their apparent freedom of choice
is actually circumscribed by environmental, legal, or political
limitations. In other words, it is unknown where and to what
extent opportunities for policy leadership exist. Much of the
richness and variety of the urban political scene will be lost unless the individual city is taken as the unit of analysis. This study
seeks to demonstrate that certain kinds of cities and certain
periods in a city's history afford the maximum opportunity for
effective policy leadership. Knowledge of this kind should provide
the background necessary for a realistic assessment of the suc-
cesses and failures of urban politics.

The policy decisions that city councils make can be approached
from both a causal and a purposive perspective. Public decision-
making is causal in that policy decisions are frequently made in
response to some problem generated by extrapolitical forces. The
very existence of city governments is a consequence of the problems and needs created by many people living closely together.
In addition to providing the basic fire, police, and sanitation
services, city governments must also respond to forces outside city
boundaries, such as a rapidly growing neighbor city, population
migration within the metropolitan region, or the proposed construction of freeways and shopping centers.

Public decision-making is purposive in that public policy decisions move toward some set of goals. The purposes underlying
city policies may reflect a variety of influences. They may reflect

residents' immediate needs or "life style preferences," or they may simply mirror the policy preferences of the city's leaders applied independently of citizen desires.

The policies a city government follows will determine whether or not it balances the disadvantages of urban life with significant advantages. A city's public life may be rich with opportunities to enhance the lives of individual citizens, or it may be lacking totally in such chances. A city may cater to its wealthy residents or to its poor ones. It may be closely attuned to the needs of its citizens or only minimally concerned about them. The alternatives a city government chooses will depend on the purposes that guide policy decisions.

From both perspectives, causal and purposive, city political leaders must be regarded as crucial intervening agents between the perception of a problem and its resolution through adopted policies. These leaders are expected to be the city's "board of directors," choosing courses of action to deal with the city's problems and guiding it toward its collective goals. Mayors and city councils are expected to make all major city policy decisions and are held accountable if their decisions prove unwise. Even in the smallest cities, councilmen must anticipate emerging problems, interpret the wishes of citizens and determine the proper course of action. In short, all the influences acting on city policy center on the policy-makers themselves. Their beliefs and interpretations are the ultimate deciding factors in the city policy process.

Some observers of urban politics argue that city policy-makers are relatively unimportant in the policy process. These observers assume that the causal factors in city policy are much more important than the purposive ones. In fact, however, the reason many cities do not meet the abstract standards critics apply to them is not that they are unable to meet the standards, but rather that they have chosen not to do so. Consequently, research into the conditions and opportunities for policy choice will be at least as rewarding as research into the consequences of particular policy choices.

In studying policy leadership from the perspective of the leaders themselves, the developmental character of public policy must also be considered. Briefly, the concept of policy used in this study views governmental action as a response to social and economic conditions that are interpreted by political leaders as pressures or challenges. A city somehow acquires or fails to acquire the capacity to affect its environment in response to changes, and this process takes place over time. How city leaders respond to environmental pressures at any given time will largely determine the directions of political change, if any, and will also affect the future characteristics of the city.

Here again city political leaders are important intervening links. When local politicians fail to perceive the crucial problems at the right moment or prove unable to react to them appropriately, these leaders often find their freedom of action seriously circumscribed on subsequent occasions. When they react correctly and guide their city in the direction that either they or the city residents have agreed upon, they prevent major future difficulties.

Plan of This Study

This study is divided into two parts, corresponding to two complementary perspectives or frameworks for city policy analysis. Part I is exploratory in character. It examines the individual city councilman as he relates to the context within which he must make policy decisions. The emphasis in Part I is on the city councilman as the focus for the pressures, constraints, and limitations in the policy process. Councilmen may or may not recognize major city problems, perceive monetary limitations on their policy decisions, or favor a highly active city government. Part I investigates these characteristics of the city councilman as decision-maker in cities of various types pursuing dissimilar policies.

Chapter 1 presents a theory of city policy that brings together the several causes of policy change in explicit and measurable form. This chapter lays the groundwork for a wide-ranging analysis of city policy by concentrating on its development over time as the result of changing causal factors.

The range of city problems perceived by councilmen is examined in chapter 2, and the underlying developmental pattern of these problems within the metropolitan region is demonstrated. This chapter also introduces the two major policy dimensions, namely, provision of amenities and city planning. Chapter 3 analyzes city tax resources and laws governing taxation as they affect city councilmen's perceptions of their freedom in making policy and budgetary decisions. Chapter 4 relates councilmen's policy preferences and budgetary behavior to the policies their cities follow.

Part II considers the city council as a purposive leadership body. This section takes the council as a whole rather than the individual councilman as its unit of analysis. Part II seeks to synthesize the city policy process from the separate elements examined in Part I by placing these elements in a causal framework and determining their relative importance to policy development. In chapter 5 a typology of policy development is used to determine the extent of policy leadership in the cities of a metropolitan region. Chapter 6 treats amenities and planning expenditures separately, building causal models of the policy process to identify those cities where policy leadership seems to be particularly important as a cause of city policy change.

Chapter 1

A Theory
of City Policy

The Metropolitan Context

According to estimates made in 1966, 64 percent of the nation's population live in a large metropolitan area.[1] As the U.S. population grows, the proportion of Americans residing in the metropolitan regions of the country will likely continue to increase. However, the majority of these persons will not live in the central cities, but in the surrounding suburbs and exurbs. Why does suburban expansion continue without any foreseeable limit? In what ways are suburbanites a part of the metropolitan economic complex? When do they begin to lose their psychological loyalties to the metropolis? All these questions are important in studying the impact of metropolitanism on cities and city policy.

Classic approaches to urban societies concentrate on the concept of "urbanism" and the importance of the dominant central city in a metropolitan region. Urbanism is a complex phenomenon involving certain psychological, social, and economic characteristics which sociologists use to distinguish the ideal types of urban and rural life styles.[2] Urban residents follow an urban life style and are oriented to the central city; rural residents

---

[1]U.S. Bureau of the Census, *Statistical Abstract of the United States: 1967* (Washington, D.C.: Government Printing Office, 1967), Table 16.
[2]Louis Wirth, "Urbanism as a Way of Life," *American Journal of Sociology* 44 (July 1938): 1–24.

follow a rural life style and are oriented to the rural community.

Research methods in disciplines like urban geography have tended to reinforce this dichotomy. The early hinterland and regional dominance studies conceived of cities as point sources of services dominating the surrounding areas,[3] while more recent regression studies have taken urban land use, a measure of the degree of "cityness" of a segment of land,[4] as the dependent variable. Here again, an area is either urban or not, depending on the use of land and the population density it supports. The analysis proceeds to examine parcels of land in concentric circles around the central city regardless of different governmental jurisdictions, seeking to predict where further increases in urban land use will occur.

Certainly there are obvious and persuasive economic reasons for metro-centered growth. Many industries and commercial activities gravitate to metropolitan centers to be near their suppliers and the businesses these in turn must service.[5] Still other businesses are "location-sensitive" and dependent on a large volume of customers and easy access to transportation for economical operation. Newspapers and perishable food retailers fall into this category.[6] Finally, new industries usually go where they can expect adequate utilities services and appropriate labor pools—resources commonly found only in or near metropolitan centers. Since the basis of urban civilization is industrial and commercial activity, the metropolitan economy should obviously be expected to follow closely changes in business activity in the metro center.

This type of analysis has been extended by transportation and exchange models applied to the different areas within a metropolis. These models usually form the backbone of planning and projection efforts for metropolitan regions. Whenever the land

---

[3]Dwight Sanderson, *Locating the Rural Community* (Ithaca: New York State College of Agriculture, 1939). See also various articles reprinted in Jack P. Gibbs, ed., *Urban Research Methods* (Princeton: Van Nostrand, 1961).
[4]F. Stuart Chapin, Jr., and Shirley F. Weiss, eds., *Urban Growth Dynamics* (New York: John Wiley & Sons, 1962).
[5]Wilbur R. Thompson, *A Preface to Urban Economics* (Baltimore: Johns Hopkins Press, 1965), Chapter 1.
[6]Edgar M. Hoover and Raymond Vernon, *Anatomy of a Metropolis* (Cambridge, Mass.: Harvard University Press, 1959), Chapters 2 and 3.

and personnel needs of employment sources and the trends in construction costs are known, the future features of a metropolitan area can be accurately predicted—if certain correct assumptions are made. Aside from the overall economic strength or weakness of the national economy, the primary assumptions that must be made are political in character. In the recent New York Metropolitan Region Study, for example, predictions were based on the assumption that political factors will continue to have only minimal effects on the growth of the region's economy and that therefore the simple projection of economic trends will provide a close approximation to the future state of the environment.[7]

Despite its plausibility, the metro-centered economic model of the metropolis has definite limitations—especially when applied to geographically extensive regions. As metropolitan growth spreads over large land areas, it begins to encompass secondary city centers with their own well-developed markets and relatively self-sufficient economic lives. Attempts have been made to extend the economic model to known multinuclear urban regions, but the outcome of sharp competition between two economically dominant centers is probably more than a simple economic calculation.

Further, in a metropolitan region with an unusual geographic configuration, like San Francisco, the shape of the region itself casts doubt on the usual assumptions regarding concentric growth patterns. A modified approach to urban spatial patterns with particular reference to the San Francisco region has recently been suggested by James E. Vance, Jr.[8] He argues that the San Francisco region is not a conurbation—a group of cities originally formed to exploit a common natural resource and since grown together—but rather a group of cities originally formed for different reasons and since grown farther apart. In fact, historically the topography of the Bay region has proved so forbidding to the circulation of population that urban development has occurred in spurts following the introduction of new forms of transportation. Thus the pedestrian and cable car residential areas are in the center, followed

[7]Raymond Vernon, *Metropolis 1985* (Cambridge, Mass.: Harvard University Press, 1960), Chapter 10.

[8]James E. Vance, Jr., *Geography and Urban Evolution in the San Francisco Bay Area* (Berkeley: Institute of Governmental Studies, 1964).

by the streetcar suburbs, the railroad suburbs, and finally the automobile areas. The geographic conditions around the Bay segregated these areas in fairly definable locations, and they retain common characteristics even to the present. The present-day descendants of these original areas form what Vance refers to as "urban realms," and journey-to-work census data reveal that they are largely self-sufficient employment and residence areas. Residents of realms close to the central city continue to be employed there, while the most common journey to work in outlying realms is from one outlying city to another.

Also, as Vance points out, from the beginning there were multiple centers to the Bay region, with San Francisco concentrating on commerce, banking, and food distribution and East Bay cities containing most of the region's industries and warehouses. Since then, dispersion of economic centers has increased, with food distribution now handled from four regional centers, retailing dispersed to large shopping centers throughout the region, new types of industry moving into the San Jose area, and commercial activity even beginning to decentralize to the north and south. Dispersion of cultural activities also continues to increase, cutting one further tie between outlying residents and the central city. What emerges is not a single-centered metropolis or even a multicentered one, but a truly noncentric urban region.

The second reason simple economic analysis breaks down is that in the far-flung suburban reaches of metropolitan regions the residents become psychologically less and less attached to the urban center, even if they do work there. A growing disparity between sociological and economic reality is apparent in the experience of metropolitan government proposals in the United States. The impetus toward metropolitan government results from the growing economic interdependence of the subareas of the region, but the failure of metropolitan government proposals to win popular approval is the product of political jealousy and psychological isolation in the suburbs.[9] Regional problems prob-

---

[9]See, for example, Walter C. Kaufman and Scott Greer, "Voting in a Metropolitan Community: An Application of Social Area Analysis," *Social Forces* 38 (March 1960): 196–204; Charles Press, "Efficiency and Economy Arguments for Metropolitan Reorganization," *Public Opinion Quarterly* 28 (Winter 1964): 584–94.

ably demand regional political mechanisms; yet differentiation and fragmentation of political loyalties becomes stronger the more the independence of small suburbs is threatened by the proposed creation of special districts or by the self-aggrandizing tactics of neighbor cities.

Residents in outlying areas become engrossed in their own concerns and seek to maintain their own distinctive life styles. They have definite ideas about grassy yards, schools, and neighbors—ideas that in many cases they protect at the personal cost of a long trip to work daily. Certain sections of a metropolitan region may also have peculiar ethnic histories. Simple economic analysis does not take these assorted factors into account in a way that reveals their impact on metropolitan politics and continuing metropolitan differentiation.

Differentiation and Economic Pressures

As a region becomes more urbanized, some activities will normally become increasingly interdependent within the region and others increasingly decentralized. The technological or economic development model predicts that both interdependence and the extent of division of labor will increase in an expanding economy. At the same time, if the classic sociological theories of Marx and Durkheim are correct, men will attach less value to their work, deriving fewer of their valued relationships from the work situation and more from their families and neighbors.[10] The relative ease of movement within metropolitan regions allows the worker to choose his residence on the basis of personal and social concerns rather than the geographical concern of being near his place of work, and the willingness of commuters to travel long distances each work day indicates that they do make residence choices on these grounds. In view of these facts we could plausibly expect that government policy toward economically interde-

---

[10]Karl Marx, *Economic and Philosophical Manuscripts,* trans. and ed. by T. B. Bottomore (New York: McGraw-Hill Book Company, 1964); Emile Durkheim, *The Division of Labor in Society,* trans. by George Simpson (Glencoe, Ill.: The Free Press, 1947), and *Suicide,* trans. by George Simpson (Glencoe, Ill.: The Free Press, 1951).

pendent activities within the metropolis would be made by regional or state governments, while city government policy would be closely related to the reasons underlying the residence choices of metropolitan area residents.

Oliver P. Williams makes similar arguments. Williams views metropolitan regions as collections of small groups of residents and the economic superstructure necessary to sustain them.[11] Each group is characterized by the choice of a distinctive life style, and members of the various groups tend to be found in clustered locations throughout the region because they wish to live in congenial environments. Life style preference is of course also influenced by an individual's economic background and the range of economic choices currently open to him.

Thus sociological typologies of cities as "upper-class residential" or "exurban" and economic classifications of cities as "residential," "balanced," or "employing" all rest on the assumption of a variety of life style preferences among residents of a metropolis. These typologies are simply alternative ways of describing the spatial results of "free" choices by individuals. Over time the differentiated land use of a region will correspond increasingly to the life style preferences of resident groups because the land use will be influenced more by the continuity of residents with similar preferences than by the decline of older "nonconforming" residents. In addition, the location choices of migrants will be increasingly restricted by the existing land uses.

There are economic complications to this model, however. Most areas will deteriorate over time. In the pure economic model the market governs both the price and the objective value of land and buildings. A dilapidated or old-fashioned building will bring less on the market than when originally built or bought and it will therefore become progressively less desirable and less economical to own and operate for its tenants. Because neighbors and potential residents are concerned about the character of the people who live around them, declining property values in one section

---

[11]Oliver P. Williams, "Life Style Values and Political Decentralization in Metropolitan Areas," in Terry N. Clark, ed., *Community Structure and Decision-Making: Comparative Analyses* (San Francisco: Chandler Publishing Company, 1968), pp. 427–40.

will usually be felt throughout the neighborhood. When property values decline for one group of owners, the properties become more attractive to some (but not all) other groups. Natural market mechanisms will assure an eventual change in character for the neighborhood.

External variables may exert an influence as well. For example, the construction of a freeway or even residential or commercial construction will affect the value of nearby parcels of land. For residential uses a new freeway may be at one and the same time a boon to commuters and a noisy imposition on others, while for commercial and warehousing uses it is definitely a benefit. Newly developed subdivisions may lower the property values of residents in adjacent high income areas while simultaneously benefiting shopping center promoters.

Though couched in terms of residential land uses, this discussion applies equally to industrial and commercial uses. For example, if a block of tenements is torn down, office buildings and high-rise apartments may be able to compete on roughly equal terms for the land vacated. The clearest illustration is that of different residential neighborhoods, however, and the tenement trail followed by various ethnic groups in the larger cities provides a highly visible marker of the process in operation.[12] Similar movements occur between cities in the metropolitan region as they go through the housing cycle outlined by Hoover and Vernon. A period of single-family home construction and growth is followed by the proliferation of multifamily dwellings, then overcrowding and downgrading, and finally thinning out, demolition, and population decline.[13]

Industrial land users, though also participants in the land market, are less mobile than other types of users. Their capitalization is greater and intrinsically less mobile, and they usually cannot compete for land once it has been utilized for high density residential or mixed residential-commercial purposes. Residential locations near industrial areas are so undesirable that low income groups are

---

[12]See the impressionistic description of this process in Samuel Lubell, *The Future of American Politics,* 2nd ed. revised (Garden City, N. Y.: Doubleday and Company, 1956), Chapter 4.
[13]Hoover and Vernon, *Anatomy of a Metropolis,* pp. 183–98.

forced to live there, but these residential uses are not sufficiently more profitable than industrial uses that they threaten to drive industry away. Consequently, old industrial areas tend to become isolated enclaves, but new industrial plants locate in a metropolis according to the economic model just outlined.

For all types of land use, however, the market's natural tendency to concentrate similar land uses geographically may be counteracted by a long-term instability in market values or unexpected fluctuations in market conditions caused by forces beyond the individual consumer's control. For this reason the congeniality model cannot by itself explain the persistence of spatially differentiated land uses.

Tiebout's theory introduces additional stability into the metropolitan land use pattern by taking into account local governmental jurisdictions and policies as well as market and congeniality factors.[14] Governmental policy is a long-standing device for working against the economic market in order to bring about certain desired results that would otherwise be impossible or uneconomical (and therefore by market assumptions unachievable). Local governments seek to modify the action of the market in ways favorable to their citizens by restricting the freedom of individual action in the market. Local residents are willing to exchange a certain measure of freedom for goals they desire but cannot attain solely through market transactions.

Referring back to Vance's description of the San Francisco region in terms of the concept of "urban realms," we can advance the following argument: the various realms were settled at different times in the history of the region by groups of people with dissimilar life style preferences, and the governmental units formed at the time of settlement followed similar policies within the several realms because they reflected the desires of the residents at that time. This is not to say that these cities and special districts continue to follow the same policies as when they were formed, but rather that they have probably gone through a similar progression of policies since their formation and have similar policies at the present time.

---

[14]Charles M. Tiebout, "A Pure Theory of Local Expenditures," *Journal of Political Economy* 64 (October 1956): 416–24.

The present boundaries of suburbs settled during the heyday of earlier transportation technologies represent both the adjustment they have made to periods of dominance of the metropolis by more advanced forms of transportation and the different life style preferences of the people who settled in the metropolis during these periods. For example, the old railroad commuter suburbs originally used for low density residential purposes are now being used for high density commercial purposes in the downtown areas—reflecting the increased land values near the central city and the shift of single family low density housing farther out on the arms of the freeway network. These areas are also seeking to attract light manufacturing to industrial parks in order to bolster the tax base and, thereby, to ease the tax burden of those city residents who still own single-family homes.

Normally, metropolitan growth in response to increasing land values in central and strategic locations manifests a roughly concentric pattern of land uses. Further, it should be possible to study the longitudinal pattern of growth within a region by examining a cross section of that region at a single point in time. For the purposes of this study, however, two important qualifications should be made. First, the geography of the San Francisco area prevented concentric development and encouraged the formation of multiple centers rather than a single one. Hence longitudinal patterns of growth took the form of realms rather than rings, and specification of the realms thereby becomes a matter concerning urban history more than geometry. Second, the continued improvement of transportation technology means that growth occurring today will not assume the spatial patterns of earlier years. In one sense it does not need to assume these patterns, because improving technology removes physical limits that previously forced urban development into particular configurations. The most obvious example of this change is the transformation of suburbia from a pattern of residences clustered around commuter train stations to one of residences dispersed across a wide area accessible only by roads.

Another reason present-day growth does not automatically assume the forms of previous years is that the economics of new transportation devices favor newer patterns over the old. In the example above, for instance, one location on a road network can be as profitable as another for a residence, and residential uses will not compete for a central point as they did in the suburban train era unless governmental policy alters the operation of natural economic forces.

These two general modifications—the development of urban realms rather than rings and the impact of new transportation technologies—should be taken into account explicitly in the case to be studied, as they may affect urban policies significantly.

A Definition of Policy

In this study "policy" is broadly defined as the relationship of a governmental unit to its environment. Because certain aspects of the operations normally carried on by city governments serve to orient them to their social and geographic setting (including their own demographic characteristics as well as those of surrounding cities), these activities are useful in identifying policies. However, a city's policy is not simply a description of all its activities. Specifying a city's policy consists in determining how the city orients itself to its environment along certain explicit and limited dimensions. Consequently, various theories relating to cities consider different kinds of relationships with the environment to be important. For example, a theory of city aesthetics could deal with city government action regarding sign ordinances, cleanup campaigns, and weed abatement allocations, and these actions would all serve to describe a city's aesthetic policy. A theory of cities as agents of social control might be concerned with the attitude of police toward minor infractions of the law or, alternatively, with the range of subjects on which the city has issued ordinances.

Either of these theories could represent a useful approach to cities, and each implies a particular theory of city policy. In both cases theoretical significance is attached to certain kinds of city government activity, and the city's policy is defined by the character of these specified activities. Because policy is a theoretical concept imposed on observed reality, a city government does not have to make specific decisions relating to the policy that it is observed to follow. Rather, city policy is inferred from observable features of city government action that can be called "policy out-comes." Policy outcomes are those decisions, programs, and expenditures undertaken by a city that seem to have relevance for its orientation toward its environment and whose presence or absence provides evidence that a particular policy is being fol-lowed. In short, policy outcomes are the means for measuring the concept of policy operationally.

According to this conception of policy, every city government possesses a wide variety of policies—whether or not they have been consciously chosen. For example, every city may be said to have an aesthetic policy even if its effect is to allow ugly signs and weed-cluttered vacant lots in the city. Viewing policy in this way frees the concept from dependence on specific decisions, treating policies instead as standing decisions about certain aspects of governmental action. As Bachrach and Baratz have suggested,[15] nondecisions may have as much impact on the lives of citizens as decisions. One of the important elements of city policy may actually be standing decisions as to what areas of social life city government is to leave unregulated.

Cities as Policy-Makers

Critics of city governments usually regard city governments as service providers. They argue that the structure of government in metropolitan areas is inadequate to provide the level of services required to meet the real needs of the population.[16]

There are several difficulties with this view. The first is a partly normative and partly technical problem—that of discovering the real needs of citizens and measuring governmental performance against these needs. The real needs of citizens could include a great many things, ranging from economic security to friendship.

---

[15]Peter Bachrach and Morton S. Baratz, "Two Faces of Power," *American Political Science Review* 56 (December 1962): 947–52, and "Decisions and Nondecisions: An Analytical Framework," *American Political Science Review* 57 (September 1963): 632–42.
[16]See, for example, the recent report from the Committee for Economic De-velopment, *Modernizing Local Government* (New York: Committee for Economic Development, 1966).

Some of these are usually not thought of as governmental responsibilities, while others may be economically unfeasible for city
governments to provide. After norms of governmental service have
somehow been established, the output of city services must be
measured to determine how satisfactorily these norms are matched
by actual programs. Although some attempts at measurement
have been made,[17] the task has proved exceptionally difficult, and
no one has tried to relate dollars-and-cents expenditures to service
norms in a systematic manner.

Criticisms of service levels usually derive from the observed
presence of problems of various kinds in urban regions. Yet, the
existence of problems does not in itself mean that they are not
being dealt with as well as possible, given the range of available
resources and the desires of citizens. Nor has it been demonstrated
that governmental reorganization will necessarily allow a more
successful attack on metro problems without endangering important political and social values, such as relative freedom of movement or personal privacy.

Further, from a purely empirical viewpoint any relationship
between the real needs of a given group of citizens and a specific
governmental unit in a metropolis is largely haphazard simply
because "government" in the abstract is parcelled among many
concrete governmental units. Each governmental unit having jurisdiction over a given piece of land in the urban complex may
provide a particular service to the people living there, but no single
unit provides for anything approaching the total real needs of this
population. A given resident may live simultaneously in a junior
college district, a high school district, an elementary school district, a regional park district, and a sewer district—each with its
own peculiar boundaries. Every one of these districts is a local
governmental unit established under state law, but most of them
are probably removed, for all practical purposes, from the direct
political control of the people they service.

The point here is simply that critics of the service levels provided
by urban governments may grossly oversimplify the situation when

---

[17]See, for example, Henry J. Schmandt and G. Ross Stephens, "Measuring
Municipal Output," *National Tax Journal* 13 (December 1960): 369–75.

they fail to distinguish between abstract concepts of government and concrete governmental units or between the aggregate of urban residents and particular groups of residents under the jurisdiction of particular governmental bodies.

This study considers city governments to be political or policy-making bodies rather than service providers. Whatever actions these governments may take that distinguish them one from another will be analyzed as policies rather than as services. A comparative analysis across a metropolitan region will reveal a high degree of variation in the policies followed by various municipalities if policies are understood as "relationships to the environment." Furthermore, policies of this kind vary both quantitatively and qualitatively from one place to another. In view of the criticism levelled at city governments and the difficulties of assessing this criticism rigorously, a logical first step in analysis would be to determine what differences do exist between city governments and what factors account for these differences. After these factors have been determined, we may be better able to see which cities are performing well and which poorly and to judge who is responsible for inadequate performance. Advocates of structural change single out only one possible source of the troubles in metropolitan areas. We may find instead that a restrictive state assessment and tax law, local government personnel, or citizen apathy are more to blame than inefficient small suburban units or structural difficulties.

Types of City Policies

The functions of local area governments can be divided into two general classes: those that are oriented to the needs of local residents and those that seek to orient the community itself to its neighboring communities. These functions may be performed either by city governments or by other local agencies. In fact, the significance of city governments in the overall picture of metropolitan government has changed markedly as metropolitan regions have developed from a scattering of cities into large urban complexes.

As urban areas expand, the cities take over as the effective layer of local government and the counties are left with the task of providing for the scattered nonincorporated areas. Since city governments were formed with limited rather than general purposes, however, county and state governments have tended to create additional special districts or public authorities to handle special services required or made possible by high density settlement instead of allowing these service responsibilities to devolve onto city governments. Provision for bridges, rapid transit, consolidated refuse collection, and water supply lines are the most common examples of these services. The effect has been to increase the range of functions performed by local government while decreasing the cities' share of these functions.

This tendency can be observed in extreme form in some Bay region cities. Many rural communities around San Francisco have resorted to incorporation as a means of protecting themselves from outside forces—developers, industries, or expansionist neighboring cities. When they do so they frequently retain a special district structure as a service provider, the city government itself carrying on only a minimum of activity (mainly, that associated with land use planning and maintenance of city offices).

This form of "defensive" incorporation in effect removes from city politics the responsibility for providing basic services. Land use issues, about which citizens usually are greatly concerned, remain in the hands of city government and are directly visible and controllable by residents through customary political channels. To these residents the most important function of city government is not the provision of services but the control of land use through restrictive zoning. Cases of defensive incorporation are infrequent, but directing attention to this tactic suggests the kind of approach that will be used in this research. Comparing various city governments' policies in relating themselves to surrounding communities will ultimately be more profitable than comparing their internal services, since the extent of the city governments' provision for these services may depend largely on the timing of incorporation.

These empirical observations can be given theoretical relevance. Oliver P. Williams distinguishes between those aspects of local government operation that are comparable across units and those

that do not readily lend themselves to comparison.[18] He treats the
metropolis as a communications system composed of a number of
interacting parts. Each part represents a group of people sharing
similar life style preferences who live closely together. In communications terms they locate near each other because they wish to
exchange compatible messages—keep up social contacts, converse
about their children, and maintain their yards—while excluding
incompatible and unpleasant signals—violence, air pollution, and
industrial noise. Industries and commercial ventures also seek
favorable surroundings and thus tend to locate near similar activities. The metropolitan system comprising these units is held together by "system maintenance" devices—transportation services,
communication networks, and utilities. These devices allow appropriate exchanges, i.e., business calls, power and water service,
and commuting arrangements among complementary groups so
that the overall system is self-sufficient and self-perpetuating.

Local governments, in this scheme, encourage area-wide control
of the communication networks but resist strongly any attempt
from outside to interfere with the life styles prevailing in their
jurisdictions. City governments adopt policies designed both to
minimize the unfavorable effects of communication links with
the outside and to maximize the internal exchange of messages.
Commonly, they utilize zoning and land use controls to prevent
the domination of external influences. As has already been suggested, new freeways bring economic pressures to bear on cities
by changing property values for various kinds of land use. By
restrictive zoning city governments may hope to prevent market
pressures from changing land use in an unfavorable direction.
Normally, other forms of intercity communication linkage such
as electrical power generation and telephone service do not produce undesirable side effects for any of the participants. Thus
city governments usually will not concern themselves with these
services as long as acceptable service levels are maintained.

Of course zoning is not entirely a negative instrument of policy.
By zoning areas for particular kinds of land use prior to their
development, a city can encourage and control its economic de-

---

[18]Oliver P. Williams, "Life Style Values."

velopment and can prevent incompatible land uses from mixing, while providing a complete range of economic activities within the city limits. Zoning policy of this kind is becoming increasingly popular in suburban areas. The suburban ideal seems to be an industrial park filled with light industry, a shopping center, single-family homes owned by well-educated high income citizens and, perhaps a few scattered apartment buildings. A "balanced" city of this type supposedly offers the maximum property tax base combined with the minimum of service requirements in an orderly and attractive community. (Whether it actually can combine these seemingly inconsistent advantages is another question entirely.)[19] What is relevant here is that city governments can be observed to produce different land use policy outputs and that we can infer from these that city governments are following certain identifiable land use policies.

Zoning decisions do not exhaust the list of city government actions that are relevant to the residents' preferred life styles. In addition to the basic services—fire and police protection and public utilities—a city government may also provide several types of amenities. In California cities these amenities may take the form of library facilities, city parks and recreation programs, and health programs of various kinds. These optional services are related to the life styles preferred by city residents, and presumably they are provided in response to desires expressed by the residents or needs perceived by local policy-makers. The theoretical variable here is defined by the extent to which the facilities for these private activities are publicly provided in a given city. In effect, this is the "public life style" of the city considered as a unit rather than the strictly private life style followed by individual citizens.

Thus, planning decisions and provision of amenities are the city policy outputs that will be of interest in this study. Both

---

[19]See the discussion of this question in Julius Margolis, "Municipal Fiscal Structure in a Metropolitan Region," *Journal of Political Economy* 65 (June 1957): 225–36; Louis K. Loewenstein, "The Impact of New Industry on the Fiscal Revenues and Expenditures of Suburban Communities," *National Tax Journal* 16 (June 1963): 113–36; Harold M. Groves and John Riew, "The Impact of Industry on Local Taxes—A Simple Model," *ibid.*, 137–45.

are related to the life styles of city residents. Zoning and planning can be considered "control" outputs, while amenities can be regarded as "adaptive" outputs. Zoning and land use policies seek to restrict the kinds of activity carried on in the city and thereby to protect city residents from neighboring land uses that would be inimical to their preferred style of living. Amenities policies seek to enrich the possibilities for individual activity in response to both the changing needs for amenities felt by urban dwellers and their decreasing ability to provide them privately. Theoretically, a city government may produce these two types of policy outputs in any proportion, corresponding to the emphasis placed by policy-makers on these two kinds of reactions to their city's environment.

Elements and Dynamics of a Policy Model

What remains to be done in this theoretical chapter is to outline the city policy process, indicating which variables are potentially important in determining how a city responds to its environment. City policies can be considered attempts to adapt to and to control the effects of environmental factors on the life styles of city residents. This basic formulation suggests two major classes of important independent variables: city and environmental characteristics on the one hand and citizen life style preferences on the other. Environmental pressures are probably the most nearly independent of the possible causes of city policy change. Thus, the basic model of policy change will link policy directly to changing environmental conditions. Complicating and intervening variables such as citizen preferences can then be inserted to increase the model's explanatory power and to make its causal mechanisms more plausible.

Metropolitan population growth tends to be concentrated in only a few areas of the metropolis at any single time. If one travels toward the geographic center of the region from these areas, he generally finds older cities that have gone through a period of rapid growth at some time in the past. If one travels away from the metro center, he finds rural, largely undeveloped land with a

scattering of unincorporated communities and a few older independent small towns that are not a part of the metropolitan
complex either economically or psychologically. Two important
changes occur when metropolitan expansion reaches a previously
undeveloped area. First, land values go up sharply and land uses
change rapidly. Second, many new residents move in and the
density of population increases sharply.

The Pressures of Growth

When land values begin to increase rapidly—or just before they
do so—the "need" for planning and land use controls becomes
greatest. Before metropolitan growth reaches an area in the metropolis, land use issues are not critical because land usage does
not change rapidly. Current land uses continue to be the most
profitable, and consequently there are no market pressures working to change land use patterns. Villages remain villages, small
merchants cling to their stores, and farms remain agricultural.
Metropolitan growth brings with it new markets and new labor
supplies, however, and new land uses do become profitable. Tract
housing and shopping centers may be planned, and industry may
want to move in. Speculators and land developers will speed up
the conversion process by centralizing and monopolizing the land
market. In California, state law also helps to spread urbanism by
requiring land valuation to be assessed according to the most
profitable potential use rather than according to actual use. When
land becomes ripe for urbanization, the property taxes go up
sharply and formerly profitable agricultural concerns cannot
compete with intensive land uses such as housing and commercial development.[20]

Regardless of the purpose of a city's land use policy—whether
it intends to control growth, to channel it, or to prevent it—the

_____

[20]Recent laws have provided exemptions for open spaces and prime agricultural lands, but by themselves these laws have not substantially altered the
spread of urbanism in California. For a summary of legal provisions in California and other states, see Thomas F. Hady and Thomas F. Stinson, *Taxation
of Farmland on the Rural-Urban Fringe,* Agricultural Economic Report No.
119 (Washington, D.C.: U. S. Department of Agriculture, 1967).

city government must at this point articulate and carry out a policy or it will very quickly be faced with the *fait accompli* of urban sprawl, which will take years to undo if in fact it can ever be undone. Later land users will throw up strong political and economic defenses against any attempts to dislodge them in favor of more rational city purposes, and the flexibility of city planners will be seriously circumscribed by previous inaction.

On the basis of these pressures alone, a large peak of planning activity (and resulting planning expenditures) should be expected at the time when the population growth rate is greatest. (Prior to this time fewer significant land use pressures existed, and after this period the land use patterns in the city will be largely set, for good or ill.) Pressures for planning may also be felt in rapidly growing areas of cities that had thought the future was under control. The spectacle of growth outrunning city planning projections is not at all uncommon.

On a remedial zoning basis the best a city can hope to do is to attempt, parcel by parcel, to eliminate nonconforming uses as the owners of these parcels either request building permits or attempt to obtain required official approval for their proposed actions. Remedial enforcement of zoning laws is not nearly as expensive as the creation of an entirely new general plan based on the different growth assumptions made necessary by unexpected metropolitan expansion. As a consequence, the pressure for planning should be expected to taper off when the city's growth slows down. Probably there will always be a need for some planning activity, because the city government cannot hope to predict correctly every eventuality and because, for monetary or political reasons, a plan cannot always be implemented at the right time. Assumptions relating to the patterns of regional expansion, the location of new freeways, and the disposition of new federal funds must constantly be re-examined to see how they affect the workability of the plan, and the plan must often be updated to correspond to what has actually transpired since it was originally adopted. However, plan revisions of this kind usually do not require as much deliberation and effort as the initial spurt of city growth called forth.

One further source of planning needs may be found in the

older cities of a region. If metropolitan expansion continues long enough, some cities in the region will go through a complete cycle of development, and their residential and commercial areas will begin to decay. This situation is likely to occur earliest in the older cities because they have been in existence longest and have gone through more changes associated with transportation technology and metropolitan expansion than have the younger cities. Urban renewal seems to be the solution, but what should be done with the renewed area is not automatically evident. Presumably some change of function is called for in the decaying areas. Otherwise, private investment would have been profitable enough to maintain the areas in their old functions. But exactly *what* change is to be made becomes a matter of public policy, because public funds are to be spent in the renewal effort. Unless planners have been remarkably prescient, they will not have foreseen the course of private development with sufficient accuracy to guide public decisions and programs. New planning efforts will be needed. The scope and the duration of urban renewal projects mean that major policy decisions must be made and that the increased planning activity involved in urban renewal reflects an actual change in city policy—at least for the period of renewal efforts.

Population Density and Urbanism

High population density exerts a pressure on city government to provide certain amenities for residents that they could not otherwise obtain. There are several underlying reasons for this pressure. Higher densities of land use occur in conjunction with higher land values. For this reason, any land-consuming facility, such as recreational fields, gardens, or parks, becomes more expensive to provide as the density of settlement increases. Some natural recreational resources such as lake fronts reach their private ownership capacity quickly and may be priced out of the private market at fairly low residential densities. Once the population density becomes high, few individuals or families can afford to pay for private recreation areas of any kind, although in low density suburbs or in rural areas they would find this task considerably less difficult.

Also, as the density of settlement increases, residents become less willing to tolerate noisy leisure activities of their neighbors. In economic terminology, important "externalities" are involved. The maintenance of separate recreational facilities in such close quarters proves difficult as well as costly, and residents are willing to forego some private amenities if suitable public amenities are made available.

The Preferences of Decision-Makers

While rapid urbanization creates pressures on city governments for increased planning activity and increased provision of urban amenities, the existence of these pressures does not by itself determine which ones will be met first or even that city governments will respond to them at all.[21] Pressures must be perceived and acted upon before they can be thought to be directly connected to policies. At best, it is metaphoric to talk of pressures brought to bear on cities or of cities "responding" to pressures by "deciding" on city policies. At bottom, all pressures must be perceived by individual decision-makers, who in turn make decisions for the legal collectivity. The actual presence of pressure for a particular policy will not prevent another policy from being followed by default if decision-makers do not perceive the pressure and act according to their perceptions. A standing policy decision will remain in effect until it is revised, and there may be a considerable time-lag between new environmental pressures and new policy responses.

City councilmen also perceive external legal and political limitations upon what they can do in responding to urban growth. Decisions made elsewhere—by other cities, county governments, the state, or the federal government—may alter the range of possible reactions to growth and slow the speed with which action can be taken.

In addition to these situations in which councilmen simply react to outside forces, there are also opportunities for councilmen to have an independent effect on city policies. Councilmen

---

21Alternative environmental assumptions are discussed in Harold and Margaret Sprout, "Environmental Factors in the Study of International Politics," *Journal of Conflict Resolution* 1 (December 1957): 309–28.

have a preferred image for their city toward which they presumably direct their energies by supporting what they think to
be appropriate policies. The personal images the councilmen
hold are assumed not to change—or at least not to change any
more rapidly than other variables in the model. Policy preferences are more directly relevant to policy outputs than are
future images. Policy preferences must be assumed to change
freely, however, because different policies may be appropriate
at different times in directing the city toward the constant image
city councilmen hold of it. For this reason, policy preferences
are treated as independent influences in the city policy process.

Available Resources

An important influence on policy is the resource base for
governmental actions. The level of resources available to a city
government will limit its policy alternatives and at the same
time will make certain policies more attractive than others. If
a city is very poor financially, its government would be foolish to
attempt a major upgrading of services—much less the providing of
new ones. If a city's assessed valuation is low, its bonding power
is limited. If a city cannot pay high salaries, it cannot expect to
get highly skilled city employees.

The cost of government services must be met in each city by
some combination of current revenues and borrowed funds, and
past borrowing must be paid off according to a rigid schedule.
Each city has a broad array of revenue sources available to it,
but each source can be expected to produce only a certain amount
of revenue. Consequently, the total amount of revenue has definite limits. The maximum amount of income a city may expect
yearly when it makes an effort to tap all available income sources
can be called its resource capability.[22]

In simple monetary terms resource capability is largely an objective factor determined by the level of actual wealth in the city,

---

[22]For an extended discussion of capabilities of political systems, see Gabriel
A. Almond and G. Bingham Powell, Jr., *Comparative Politics: A Developmental Approach* (Boston: Little, Brown, 1966).

tax rebates from county and state governments, and federal or state grants. But resource capability is also a subjective concept in that city residents will differ on how high a tax rate they are willing to tolerate, and city councils will vary in how much reliance they are willing to place on grants and rebates. Resource capability is a potential limit in the city environment, but its limiting effect must be interpreted by citizens and officials before it becomes a factor in the policy-making process. City resources are more subjective than other environmental factors precisely because they are politically controversial. Next to land use decisions, tax decisions are the most visible and the most difficult to make because city politicians must weigh more factors against one another than in "nonpolitical" decisions such as those relating to fire truck purchases or traffic ordinances.

Gasoline and sales tax revenues are largely predictable, barring slumps in the national economy; the marginal variations in revenues from year to year will therefore depend closely on property tax rate decisions made at the city level. Special and nonrecurring grants may enable a city to undertake unusual expenditure programs for a year or two, but the transient nature of these funds suggests that the programs they make possible do not become a part of continuing city policy. Cities are more likely to react opportunistically to the availability of grants than to expect and approve of them on a regular basis. For this reason taxes and tax decisions loom large in the resource base of a city. Nevertheless, the objective measures of city tax base, the variety of tax resources, and the availability of grants should be supplemented by subjective measures of resources as perceived by city decisionmakers—how much attention they pay to tax rates, how much constraint they feel from tax ceilings, and how much they think city residents are willing to spend.

Citizen Demands and Preferences

In studies of state and national politics, especially in legislative studies, constituency characteristics are always considered important from a theoretical standpoint. Constituency relations are no less significant in the study of cities; in fact, some scholars

have argued that they are especially important in small governing units such as cities.[23]

In several respects citizen desires can be thought of as an empirical linkage between environmental pressures and policy outputs. For example, the economic pressures exerted on lower
income residents by increasing urban density may force them out
of the private amenities market faster than upper income groups,
giving rise to greater political pressures for amenities in low income cities than in high income ones.

Also, the urban or rural character of constituents might be
considered as the linkage between urbanism and amenities policies. Classic sociological theory postulates two ideal types of life
style. Rural existence is characterized by "traditional" relationships—face-to-face contact, family and group-centered living, and
traditional leadership and deference patterns.[24] Urban existence
as the counterpart ideal type involves "modern" relationships—
impersonal contact, individual-centered living, and achievement
as the source of leadership and deference.[25] Urbanization of an
area brings with it an influx of people of the modern type who,
in contrast to the older traditional residents, are inclined toward
a public life style characterized by a wide circle of contacts,
frequent travel, and frequent use of mass media.[26] As a consequence, the balance of life style preferences within the urbanizing community will change from "traditional" to "modern."
Since moderns are more inclined to consume public goods of all
kinds than are traditionals, the population influx will put increased pressure on the city government to provide amenities

---

[23]See, for example, Robert C. Wood, *Suburbia, Its People and Their Politics*
(Boston: Houghton Mifflin, 1958), Chapter 4. A similar argument is made in
Grant McConnell, *Private Power and American Democracy* (New York: Alfred
A. Knopf, 1966).

[24]See Robert Redfield, *Peasant Society and Culture* (Chicago: University of
Chicago Press, 1956).

[25]See Louis Wirth, "Urbanism as a Way of Life," *American Journal of Sociology*
44 (July 1938): 1–24.

[26]The communications aspect of urban life is emphasized in Richard L. Meier,
A Communications Theory of Urban Growth (Cambridge, Mass.: M.I.T.
Press, 1962).

of urban life such as parks and recreation areas, libraries, and health programs.

This formulation is not completely satisfactory, however. Changes in citizen demands may not immediately follow a change in environmental characteristics, especially when there is little population turnover in the city in question. Similarly, the urban-rural dichotomy may explain some of the pressures exerted by citizens for amenities in extremely low or extremely high density cities, but within the vast collection of medium density suburbs it is less relevant. Amenities policies in these cities can probably be explained in large part only by viewing citizen preferences as independent life style variations resulting from the conscious self-selection of neighbors. These life style variations may be assumed, at least for theoretical purposes, to be substantially independent of income: the variations would give rise to differing levels of demand for public amenities even among city residents with similar socioeconomic characteristics.

In view of these arguments, it is desirable in the policy process model to allow for independent effects or even contradictory relationships between citizen demands and environmental pressures. Finally, the tolerance of city residents for increased taxes is also an important limit on city policies that is not obviously related to either population growth or urbanization. Therefore, citizen preferences will be assumed to be independent variables in the short run. In the long run, city policy and citizen preferences will probably reach a mutual accommodation because existing policies will form a part of the city "packages" among which newcomers or migrating residents will choose according to their own life style preferences.

A Note on the Concept of Development

The concept of development will be used in several ways in this study. There is a developmental sequence for cities within the metropolitan region, and there is a developmental sequence of city policy. Each sequence has recognizable stages and periods of transition between stages. Development consists of changes in city characteristics or city government policy that can be described in terms of the stages of a developmental sequence. Thus, not all changes constitute development, but only those that alter the relevant variables sufficiently and for a long enough period of time so that at least two distinct stages in a developmental sequence can be identified.

Specifically, city development within the metropolitan region consists of increases in the density of land use and in the diversity of economic activities located within the city. The three broad stages of city development correspond roughly to fringe cities, suburbs, and core area cities. Fringe cities are low in population density and low in economic diversity, being primarily agricultural or exclusively residential in character. Suburbs are more densely settled, and they may also be more diversified if they have shopping centers and industrial parks. Core cities are the most densely settled and the most diversified, often having large central business districts and industrial areas, a variety of residential areas—single-family homes, high-rise apartments, tenements—and many public buildings serving a large portion of the metropolitan region. Urbanizing cities represent a transitional phase between fringe and suburban stages, and industrializing suburbs are intermediate between suburbs and core area cities.

At any given moment a cross section of a metropolitan region will reveal some cities of each type. In any given period of time some cities will be moving from one stage to another, although movement will probably occur slowly except at the fringes of the region. This sequence of stages constitutes genuine development because increases in city density and diversity are generally irreversible. Once a city acquires industry, the factories are likely to remain. Once an area is settled in apartments, single-family homes will not likely reappear. Not every city will go through all stages of course. Evidence for the existence of a developmental sequence consists of the movement of cities between adjacent stages—fringe cities become commuter suburbs, railroad suburbs acquire shopping centers and industrial parks, and core cities build more high-rise apartments and office buildings.

The conditions of density and diversity at each stage and the rate of population growth associated with the stages and the

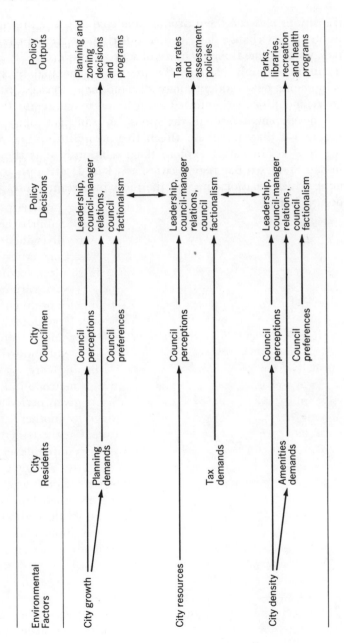

Figure 1-1
Variables in a Model of City Policy

transitions between them produce the characteristic pressures for public policy change described in this chapter. Actual changes in policy may come from a variety of sources, however. City governments may simply react to the pressures generated by city development, new residents may demand new services from city government, or newly elected councilmen may attempt to direct city development through the sponsorship of particular policies. Figure 1–1 diagrams these alternative possibilities. The remaining chapters in Part I explore these relationships as they occur in San Francisco Bay region cities, and Part II attempts to determine which relationships are the most important causes of city policy change.

Chapter 2

Cities, Councilmen, and Policy Problems

Certain characteristics of cities and their environments provide an impetus for city government action: if some aspect of city life does not meet the standards the community or its councilmen have implicitly set for it, a new governmental program or policy decision will be needed. New programs will not be initiated nor decisions made, however, until the city councilmen become aware of the need for them. This linkage between problem and action is absolutely essential for effective city policy-making.

The next two chapters explore several kinds of relationships between councilmen and their environments in the San Francisco Bay region. The first and most obvious of these relationships is the councilmen's perception of problems in their cities. "Problems" demand the most direct and immediate action by city councilmen. Consequently, they are probably the strongest influence on the city policy process.

Some problems may be the result of city development. If amenities and planning policies are relevant to a city's patterns of development, the pressures accounting for development should appear in the policy process as a characteristic series of problems to which city policy-makers respond in making decisions. Testing this hypothesis requires classifying the cities in the Bay region according to their position in the city developmental sequence presented in chapter 1. The basic elements of this classification are the city's growth rate and its population density.

In addition to these two elements, the concept of urban realms also can be used to distinguish among cities in the same metropolitan region. The urban realm typology, mentioned briefly in the last chapter, is based on the historical sequence of settlement and on the means of transportation prevailing when the various segments of the metropolitan region were first urbanized. Consequently, the urban realm typology can serve both as a rough indicator of a sequence of ecological development within the region and as a measure of the city life style established by the groups who first settled in the various areas of the region. Basically, then, the urban realm classification represents the history of development of a city, while growth rate and population density reveal the differences between cities classified in the same urban realm.

By using both the urban realm typology and growth rate and density characteristics of a city, we are testing the hypothesis that the developmental history of a city is an important factor in that city's policy process. A city's developmental history may not be all-determining, because redevelopment is always possible. For example, some settled railroad suburbs are acquiring industrial parks and apartment buildings, thereby changing in character from densely settled, single family, high income suburbs to more diversified cities with balanced economic bases. This new city-type cannot be described adequately by its history alone, but the addition of growth rate and density as measures of the developmental pressures currently operating will serve to distinguish it from railroad suburbs that have not undergone this change of character.

The Realms of the San Francisco Region

Bay region cities can be placed in six distinct realms through the use of historical accounts and current census data.[1] These realms are:

1. traditional core areas and preautomotive industrial areas;
2. traditional or "prairie" residential areas—old streetcar suburbs;

---

[1]This classification is based on James E. Vance, Jr., *Geography and Urban Evolution in the San Francisco Bay Area* (Berkeley: Institute of Governmental

3. railroad suburbs—older, high income commuter areas;
4. postwar automotive ("noncentric") housing and industrial areas;
5. urbanizing areas and areas of imminent urbanization; and
6. fringe areas—older cities at the periphery of the metropolitan complex and isolated from the metropolitan economy.

Broadly speaking, these realm categories summarize the several aggregate characteristics of cities that may be important in the policy decisions their city councils make. These characteristics are shown in Table 2–1.

The table shows clearly that the urban realm classification does separate cities into distinctive groups. Population density is most closely related to the realms in the order listed, with central areas being densely settled and fringe areas being very sparsely settled. Core cities themselves show a slightly lower average density than prairie residential cities, because a few low density industrial or residential enclaves remain in core areas.

Conforming to the theory outlined in chapter 1, population growth is concentrated in noncentric and urbanizing cities, with both core and fringe areas growing very slowly. Unurbanized land within city boundaries, which provides the space necessary for population growth, is also concentrated in these rapidly growing areas of the region. Urbanizing cities are annexing land most rapidly, but their slightly lower rate of population growth shows that the land is largely undeveloped and unpopulated.

Finally, the table also relates the urban realm classification to social characteristics of the city residents such as median income and occupational status level. As a group, the railroad suburbs and the noncentric residential areas fit the traditional image of affluent suburbia, having the highest family income level and the highest proportion of white collar workers in the region. At the other end of the scale, the core cities and urbanizing cities show

Studies, 1964). Several of Vance's fringe cities have been recoded as urbanizing in order to bring the classification into agreement with conditions at the time of council interviewing. The distinction between residential and industrial noncentric cities was based on 1965 land use data: cities with 10% or less of their land area in commercial and industrial use were designated residential and the rest were classed as industrial. The geography of these urban realms is indicated by the map in Appendix A.

Table 2-1
Demographic Characteristics of Urban Realms in the San Francisco Bay Region

Urban realm	Population/ sq. mi. 1965	% Pop. growth 1960–1965	% Land undeveloped 1965	% Area increase 1961–1965	Median family income 1960	% White collar 1960	% Land area industrial/ commercial 1965
Core cities (N = 7)	4373	4.8	30.5	17.6	$5997	39.7	48.0
Prairie residential (N = 6)	5748	14.0	22.3	13.8	8147	48.8	24.3
Railroad suburbs (N = 23)	3353	22.4	27.6	11.4	9860	62.6	7.9
Noncentric residential (N = 13)	3485	30.2	43.8	38.2	8244	57.8	8.1
Noncentric industrial (N = 15)	3032	69.8	62.0	26.3	7184	42.4	30.8
Urbanizing cities (N = 11)	2086	36.4	63.9	59.4	5950	46.8	9.5
Nonmetro cities (N = 14)	1825	6.8	39.5	13.0	7122	48.8	3.8
All cities (N = 89)	3163	29.1	42.5	24.2	7920	51.9	16.3

the lowest income and occupational levels. The figures for land usage demonstrate that these characteristics of the cities' residents are also strongly related to patterns of economic activity in the respective cities, but that the relationship is not complete. Core cities have the highest percentage of industrial and commercial land use and nearly the lowest median family income, but the next most industrial and commercial cities, the prairie and non-centric industrial groups, are relatively high in income. The lowest group on income, urbanizing cities, is also low in industrialization rather than high.

City characteristics, even within this one metropolitan region, apparently do not fall along a single continuum. Rather, a number of distinctive types of cities emerge and maintain themselves over long periods of time. The urban realm classification seems to provide a convenient and intuitively understandable way of summarizing most of these types.

The Range of Perceived City Problems

In view of the wide variety of cities in the Bay region, one would expect to find a correspondingly wide range of problems mentioned by the councilmen in these cities. For this reason the questions in the interview schedule relating to city problems were left completely open. The basic question asked was

> Mr. Councilman, before talking about your work as a councilman and the work of the council itself, we would like to ask you about some of the problems facing this community. . . . In your opinion, what are the two most pressing problems here in (city)? Why is (first problem) a problem here in (city)? Why is (second problem) a problem?

The councilmen could—and did—discuss anything that was on their minds when the interviews took place. After most of the interviews had been completed, a code was developed that first placed each of the problem responses for each respondent into one of several broad categories and then attempted to record the substance of each problem as exactly as possible. The reasons given for each problem were coded similarly.

Table 2–2 shows the two most frequently mentioned problems for each council, and Table 2–3 depicts the two most common reasons mentioned by each council for these problems.[2] The two tables demonstrate that different problems do arise in different parts of the metropolitan region and that the nature of these problems is related to the position of the city in the sequence of development hypothesized in chapter 1. These points can be seen most easily by using the noncentric cities as a basis for comparison. Taken together, these cities comprise the postwar settlement areas that house the new aerospace plants and their employees and have been responsible for the phenomenal growth of the Bay region since the mid-1950's. Numerically they are the largest group of cities, and they display the broadest range of problems.

The kinds of problems perceived by councilmen in cities on either side of this noncentric group differ markedly. Social, redevelopment, and urban renewal problems predominate in core areas, while intergovernmental and planning problems are especially important in urbanizing cities. These kinds of problems clearly indicate the difference between initial growth—the experience of fringe areas—and urban decay and redevelopment—the plight of the core cities. Streets are a problem in the old streetcar suburbs where streetcars no longer run and in railroad commuter suburbs settled before the widespread use of automobiles. In fringe areas where, according to the earlier hypothesis, urbanization has not yet become important, the provision of traditional services proves to be most troublesome.

The reasons councilmen cite to explain their cities' problems relate less clearly to the position of the city within the region, but certain reasons apparently apply to major segments of the

---

[2]To determine the two most frequently mentioned problems for each council, all problem mentions from a given council were used. The two problems with the greatest number of mentions were designated as the most frequently mentioned problems. Where ties for the second most frequently mentioned problem occurred, the two or three problems so tied were included with deflated scores totaling one "mention." Thus each council was weighted equally, having the equivalent of two problems. Where "no problems" was a frequently mentioned response, however, that city is represented in Table 2–2 by only one problem response. The two most frequently mentioned reasons for each council were coded similarly.

region. In the urbanizing and nonmetropolitan cities on the edges of the region—those faced with imminent or future growth—the area-wide magnitude of the problems and the lack of leadership and planning are the most important reasons cited. These cities are not yet growing very rapidly, but their city councils apparently recognize the problems that growth will bring. As one councilman remarked,

> We need different leadership, one that's more forward-looking as to development of the city as a whole. . . . The administration's attitude toward development is anything but understanding—there's too much red tape and delay. (Councilman 60504)

Moving in toward the center of the region, we find that city growth is by far the most important reason mentioned in noncentric industrial cities, the group experiencing the fastest growth. At the same time, councils in these cities complain that their citizens are apathetic to city problems. A number of councilmen suggested that growth and apathy went hand in hand: the influx of new residents, inexperienced and uninterested in city government, frequently made the solution of city problems doubly difficult.

In the center of the region lack of adequate money is the most commonly mentioned reason for the existence of problems. Surprisingly, this is rated by councilmen as more important than the area-wide character of problems. Table 2–2 indicates that the problems facing these cities are the ones typical to decaying central cities anywhere in the United States: housing, race relations, unemployment, urban renewal, industrial development, and poor streets. These are complex problems, as the councilmen in these cities recognize:

> One of our problems is finding employment for the influx of people from other areas. We should eliminate the so-called social unrest of minority groups—employment would do this. . . . There is not much awareness of what the solutions will be. We all feel that subsidies from the federal, state, and county governments, while they have helped, have not done the job. (Councilman 10605)

> We need industrialism, to broaden the tax base with industry. This has been a concern for years. The tax structure of this city, with the influx of people who are demanding services, results in

Table 2-2

Two Most Frequently Mentioned Problems, by Council and Realm,
in the San Francisco Bay Region

Type of problem	Core cities (N = 6)	Prairie residential (N = 6)	Railroad suburbs (N = 22)	Noncentric residential (N = 13)	Noncentric industrial (N = 14)	Urbanizing cities (N = 10)	Nonmetro cities (N = 13)
Social: housing, race relations, unemployment	50%	25%	2%	10%	4%	5%	4%
Urban renewal, industrial development	30	17	5	8	21	15	4
Streets, freeways		25	21	11	15	5	4
Paying for services			19	4	11		8
Zoning		17	16	23	4		13
Amenities	10		10	10	10	5	4
Intergovernmental relations, city government unity		8	5	11	21	30	13
Planning			12	12	4	15	17
Basic services	10	8	10	11	10	25	33
	100%	100%	100%	100%	100%	100%	100%
(Number of problem responses)	(10)	(12)	(42)	(26)	(27)	(20)	(24)

Table 2-3
Two Most Common Reasons for Problems, by Council and Realm, in the San Francisco Bay Region

Type of reason	Core cities (N = 6)	Prairie residential (N = 6)	Railroad suburbs (N = 22)	Noncentric residential (N = 13)	Noncentric industrial (N = 14)	Urbanizing cities (N = 10)	Nonmetro cities (N = 13)
Lack of money	30%	11%	7%	6%	4%	3%	4%
Citizen apathy	13	8	2	12	13	2	
Lack of planning or leadership	22	30	33	19	23	33	27
Area-wide problem, requiring cooperation of groups or other levels of government	15	28	24	24	4	24	32
City growth	10	7	25	23	44	28	21
Old facilities	10	16	9	16	12	10	16
	100%	100%	100%	100%	100%	100%	100%
(Number of reason responses)	(10)	(12)	(43)	(26)	(26)	(19)	(24)

increased costs, and there is a limited amount of land. Industries who want to expand find that the land costs too much. We don't offer what industry wants. (Councilman 11203)

Despite the apparent complexity of the problems, councilmen see a lack of money as the primary barrier to their solution. Citizen apathy and a lack of leadership or planning are also involved, but they seem to be secondary factors.

Table 2–2 shows that the noncentric and railroad suburbs, midway in the hypothesized sequence of development, face a variety of problems. Table 2–3 shows that one of the important reasons mentioned by councilmen for these diverse problems is city growth. Growth strains the capacity of all city services at the same time that it creates a need for new ones. Thus, not surprisingly, cities that have recently gone through a period of growth often have a backlog of problems of all kinds. A statement by a councilman in one of these cities illustrates the situation clearly:

> We need proper planning and building of capital improvements and the acquisition of property. The area is growing so rapidly and is expected to grow more yet. If we don't decide where to put buildings in the next 10 to 20 years, the land will be used up, and the land we have to buy will be very expensive. We need to build roads, put in parks, sewage and water facilities to handle our future needs. (Councilman 51204)

The effect of city growth can also be demonstrated by looking at the number of problems mentioned by councilmen in the various groups of cities. Table 2–4 shows that the growth rate and the diversity of city problems are related. The two groups of cities growing at the slowest rates (core and nonmetro) possess the fewest problems, while cities in the middle of the hypothesized sequence of city development, where most of the region's growth is taking place, have the greatest number of problems.

In summary, the three broad areas of the metropolis—core, suburbs, and fringe—appear to have different sets of problems. Many reasons, such as the deterioration of old facilities, the lack of adequate planning, and the area-wide nature of these problems, are important in nearly all parts of the region, but others

Table 2–4
Number of Kinds of Problems Mentioned,
by Council and Realm

Realm	Cities with 2, 3, or 4 problems	Cities with 5, 6, 7, or 8 problems	(Cities)
Core cities	50%	50%	(6)
Prairie residential	33	67	(6)
Railroad suburbs	41	59	(22)
Noncentric residential	23	77	(13)
Noncentric industrial	43	57	(14)
Urbanizing cities	40	60	(10)
Nonmetro cities	69	31	(13)
All cities	43%	57%	(84)

are prominent at specific points in the city's development. Thus, the urban realm typology does classify cities within the same metropolitan region in a manner that will be useful for policy research.

Planning and Zoning as Policy Problems

We can go beyond this outline view of city problems to look at some of them in more detail. Of special interest here are those policy problems that are closely related to city life styles. In terms of the categories derived from interviews with councilmen, these include planning, zoning, and amenities. If the conditions created by metropolitan expansion are important for the life style policy decisions made by city governments, life style policy problems should occur in cities with certain kinds of environmental characteristics. To be more specific, planning and zoning problems should be expected when a city passes from a relatively static condition to one of rapid change, or when city policy diverges markedly from the city type dictated by real estate market conditions. Amenities problems should arise when a city has developed beyond the point of private provision of amenities but has not yet met its amenities needs through public action.

The urban realm typology describes cities according to their means of settlement and general life style, but it does not by itself indicate which cities are attempting to develop counter to market conditions nor does it specify very closely the pressures for amenities spending. A better test of the model of city policy outlined in chapter 1 can be made by supplementing the urban realm classification with other measures that should be related to life style policy problems.

Planning and zoning are similar in that both involve legal action by cities seeking to control their development through land use regulations. In the terms used by councilmen to describe city problems, however, planning and zoning are different approaches to controlling the environment. Generally, councilmen seem to be concerned either about anticipating and providing for growth and development of large segments of the city (planning) or about preserving the desirable character of the city by preventing redevelopment and change (zoning). Some interview excerpts will show the difference between these two orientations:

Planning—

To some degree the political philosophy of the council can control the city. For example, there are population and traffic studies, Plan 701. . . . I want this city to be a model city for progressive planning and environmental adaptation, give it character and identity. . . . (Councilman 11504)

I think perhaps our most important problem would be a lack of planning. A master plan or general plan. A general plan is a policy statement of what kind of city it's going to be. Without some common consensus you get a helter-skelter arrangement. (Councilman 41804)

Zoning—

Our major problem is the preservation of beauty, including landscaping, slope policy, proper development of land, and holding down the density so that the character of the community is not changed. A developer will try to put as many buildings on a lot as he can, cut the size of the lots as much as possible. He will cut and fill if he is allowed to do so. This has to be controlled. (Councilman 51201)

We need to conserve the essential character of the city. . . . . This is substantially a mature city and, as far as land use, fully developed city. There is always the possibility of subdividing lots. It isn't a question of just holding the status quo, but it is a question of preventing people from creating such high density that they destroy the values, both material and aesthetic, through the high density development. (Councilman 50501)

The distinction between these two kinds of planning activity should be associated with different stages of city development and therefore different aggregate city characteristics. For example, if the cities are classified according to rate of population increase, as shown in Table 2–5, the effect of growth within realms can be examined. The patterns are not entirely clear because they are not consistent from realm to realm. Planning simply is not seen as a problem by councilmen in core and industrial cities. In suburbs and fringe areas, however, planning is mentioned frequently in cities whose population is growing more than 2 percent a year. Thus, if planning problems are generated simply by city growth, only a moderate rate of growth is necessary to alert city councilmen to the need for more planning activities.

Councilmen in slowly growing cities mention zoning as a city problem more often than councilmen in rapidly growing cities. This relationship holds only for core and suburban areas, however. At least some rapidly growing cities in the fringe areas of the region are troubled by zoning problems. We can tentatively conclude from Table 2–5 that zoning is a form of environmental control undertaken by city governments when residents feel their life style threatened by nearby development, but that a low growth rate is not always necessary for zoning to be a city problem. Comments by city councilmen support this interpretation linking zoning problems to developmental pressures:

We try to keep the town from being divided into less than one-acre pieces. With the population increase in the area, appreciation of property in the area, you will always find people who will take

Table 2–5
Perception of Planning and Zoning Problems, by Urban Realm and Growth Rate

Table entries are the percentage of councilmen in each cell (total number shown in parentheses) who mentioned the given problem.

Realm	PLANNING			ZONING		
	Population increase, 1960–1965			*Population increase, 1960–1965*		
	50% or more	10–49%	under 10%	50% or more	10–49%	under 10%
Core, prairie residential, and noncentric industrial	7 (41)	6 (52)	8 (51)	7 (41)	6 (52)	17 (51)
Railroad suburbs and noncentric residential	27 (33)	31 (80)	15 (55)	21 (33)	21 (80)	33 (55)
Urbanizing and nonmetropolitan cities	30 (10)	33 (60)	16 (50)	20 (10)	8 (60)	20 (50)
All cities	18 (84)	25 (192)	13 (156)	14 (84)	12 (192)	24 (156)

advantage of a split-up. . . . There are pressures from our proximity to San Francisco, and there will be more pressures when the rapid transit comes in. . . . (Councilman 41903)

One of our problems is preventing an annexing larger city from totally engulfing the surrounding unincorporated area. That city has leveled the hills in its area right off, and we don't want it to happen here. Those of us who moved here did so because it was a beautiful valley. We would like to develop those areas to preserve natural resources and their natural beauty. Our neighboring city has shown that commercialism has taken over planning. (Councilman 21005)

More direct evidence in support of this interpretation of zoning problems can be derived from aggregate indicators of citizen life styles. For example, the median market value of owned homes in a city can be used to characterize the life style of city residents. The higher the value of houses, the greater the residents' investment is—and the more they wish to retain an exclusive, low density residential environment without unsightly commercial or industrial activity. Table 2–6 indicates that the median value of homes is not related to city planning problems, because a similar pattern of responses appears at all levels of house value. However, nearly half of the councilmen in slowly growing high value cities mentioned zoning problems, a proportion unmatched by any other group of cities. In other words, the cities where zoning is a matter of council concern are upper income cities that are not growing or changing very much but are trying to prevent land use changes from being imposed on them from outside.

The hypothesis that zoning is a response to perceived outside pressures is further supported by cross tabulations with relative income levels, shown in Tables 2–7 and 2–8. Zoning is perceived to be a problem in cities whose neighbors are of a lower income level and not a problem in cities whose neighbors are of a similar or higher income level.[3] This relationship holds when city population density (Table 2–7) or the rate of land annexation by

---

[3]Neighboring cities were defined as those with a boundary in common. They were coded as lower in family income if at least one had a median family income at least 15% lower than the income level of the city in question.

Table 2–6
Perception of Planning and Zoning Problems,
Controlling for Median House Value and Growth Rate

*Table entries are the percentage of councilmen in each
cell (total number shown in parentheses) who mentioned
planning as a city problem.*

Median value of owned homes, 1960	Population increase, 1960–1965		
	50% or more	10–49%	under 10%
$18,000 or more	21 (14)	28 (67)	10 (59)
$14,600–$17,999	17 (46)	30 (57)	9 (23)
Under $14,600	21 (19)	16 (67)	14 (56)

*Table entries are the percentage of councilmen in each
cell (total number shown in parentheses) who mentioned
zoning as a city problem.*

Median value of owned homes, 1960	Population increase, 1960–1965		
	50% or more	10–49%	under 10%
$18,000 or more	14 (14)	24 (67)	47 (59)
$14,600–$17,999	17 (46)	2 (57)	13 (23)
Under $14,600	11 (19)	9 (67)	4 (56)

neighboring cities (Table 2–8) is controlled.[4] Taken together,
these tables suggest that the perception of possible threats to
life styles (indicated here by the proximity of lower income

---

[4] For Table 2–7 the highest land annexation rate of neighboring cities was
used. The calculations for land annexation rate were based on land area
estimates made in 1961 and 1965 by the California State Division of Highways.

Table 2–7

Perception of Zoning Problems,
Controlling for Relative Income Level and Population Density

*Table entries are the percentage of councilmen in each
cell (total number shown in parentheses) who mentioned
zoning as a city problem.*

Population density in persons per square mile, 1965	Income level of neighboring cities, 1960	
	Same or higher	Lower
4000 or more	5 (93)	18 (34)
2000–3999	16 (91)	18 (28)
Under 2000	9 (67)	48 (50)
All cities	10 (251)	31 (112)

Table 2–8

Perception of Zoning Problems,
Controlling for Relative Income Level
and Surrounding Area Growth

*Table entries are the percentage of councilmen in each
cell (total number shown in parentheses) who mentioned
zoning as a city problem.*

Increase in land area of neighboring cities, 1961–1965	Income level of neighboring cities, 1960	
	Same or higher	Lower
30% or more	15 (128)	25 (51)
4–29%	7 (60)	39 (41)
Under 4%	5 (63)	30 (20)

groups) is at least as important in calling forth a zoning policy
response as actual threatening behavior (indicated by active annexation by surrounding cities) or susceptibility to unfavorable
development (low density land use in the city itself).

In summary, there appear to be two general classes of control
policy for cities. Planning is a response to the pressures imposed
on a city when it first becomes subject to metropolitan expansion.
Zoning is a response to external pressures felt by cities that have
never undergone significant expansion and wish to prevent it,
or by cities already developed and faced with possible redevelopment and downgrading as a result of the same pressures of metropolitan expansion.

Amenities Problems and City Values

City governments are likely to undertake the public provision
of amenities in response to the impracticality of private amenities
provision in densely settled urban areas. The analysis so far has
not demonstrated this relationship, but it should be demonstra-
ble by combining density and urban realm classifications. Table
2–9 reveals no support for the hypothesis, however. Amenities
problems are mentioned more frequently in the noncentric cities
than elsewhere, but within realms city density is not related to
amenities in any consistent manner.

Some confirmation can be given to the supposed effect of population density on amenities needs by looking at density changes
over a five-year period. At least some of the cities where population density has increased significantly since 1961 should experience an increased demand for public parks and similar
services, while cities whose density has remained the same or declined should experience a constant or declining demand for
public amenities. This is true, as shown in Table 2–10, for cities
at all density levels in 1965. Apparently the amenities problems
perceived by city councilmen reflect *changes* in environmental
pressures more closely than they do the general level of these
pressures. For amenities problems, an increase in city population
density is more important than high density in itself.

If public provision of amenities is an expression of city life
style, councilmen's concern for amenities should be related to the

Table 2–9
Perception of Amenities Problems,
Controlling for Urban Realm and Population Density

Table entries are the percentage of councilmen in each cell (total number shown in parentheses) who mentioned amenities as a city problem.

Realm	Population density in persons per square mile in 1965		
	4000 or more	2000–3999	Under 2000
Core, prairie residential, and noncentric industrial	12 (77)	15 (33)	14 (35)
Railroad suburbs and noncentric residential	26 (47)	21 (68)	11 (53)
Urbanizing and nonmetropolitan cities	0 (5)	8 (61)	15 (54)
All cities	16 (129)	15 (162)	13 (142)

preferences of citizens in addition to the hypothesized pressures for public amenities exerted by population density. Median family income, one measure of citizen life style, is positively related to council concern for amenities in cities of all densities of settlement, as indicated by Table 2–11. However, the value of owned homes, another measure of life style, is not related to a concern for amenities at any level of population density, according to the evidence presented in Table 2–12.

The probable explanation for this discrepancy between measures is that they reveal different aspects of citizen life style. Both house value and family income should be indicators of citizen desires for "exclusivity," but expensive homes and their attendant large private yards can serve as private substitutes for public

Table 2–10
Perception of Amenities Problems,
Controlling for Density Change
and Population Density

*Table entries are the percentage of councilmen in each
cell (total number shown in parentheses) who mentioned
amenities as a city problem.*

Change in density, 1961–1965	Population density in persons per square mile in 1965		
	4000 or more	2000–3999	Under 2000
Increase	19 (104)	19 (77)	17 (59)
No change, or decrease	4 (25)	11 (80)	7 (66)
All cities	16 (129)	15 (157)	12 (125)

Table 2–11
Perception of Amenities Problems,
Controlling for Median Family Income
and Population Density

*Table entries are the percentage of councilmen in each
cell (total number shown in parentheses) who mentioned
amenities as a city problem.*

Median family income in 1960	Population density in persons per square mile in 1965		
	4000 or more	2000–3999	Under 2000
$7800 or more	24 (45)	22 (41)	20 (50)
$6800–$7799	18 (51)	13 (53)	13 (23)
Under $6800	3 (33)	13 (63)	13 (46)

Table 2–12
Perception of Amenities Problems,
Controlling for Median House Value
and Population Density

Table entries are the percentage of councilmen in each cell (total number shown in parentheses) who mentioned amenities as a city problem.

Median value of owned homes, 1960	Population density in persons per square mile in 1965		
	4000 or more	2000–3999	Under 2000
$18,000 or more	21 (33)	15 (47)	17 (60)
$14,600–$17,999	13 (62)	14 (42)	4 (24)
Under $14,600	18 (34)	16 (68)	19 (41)

parks to a greater extent than can a high family income by itself. Therefore, although both large property owners and high income groups presumably value the urban amenities represented by parks and recreation areas, owners of extensive property can provide these for themselves while high income groups—to the extent that they live in areas where it is impossible to maintain sufficiently large private land holdings—will seek parks and recreational facilities through city government action. If this hypothesis is true, councilmen's concern for amenities arises at least partly, though not entirely, from their city's ability to pay for them. Unfortunately, councilmen seldom describe their concern for amenities in terms that would either confirm or deny this explanation, so that it must remain merely plausible but unproven.

Conclusions

Great care should be exercised in interpreting the findings reported in this chapter. By asking councilmen to name the two most pressing problems in their city, we have not exhausted the range of problems that concern them; nor have we necessarily determined the level of planning or amenities their cities provide. Amenities could be as problematic in central cities as in others, for example, but central cities might also have other more pressing problems about which their councilmen would more readily respond. Further, the level of amenities provided publicly may be as high in central cities as elsewhere without amenities being a very important matter for council concern.[5]

The most that can be concluded with certainty from the interview data is the period of development during which a given problem is most prominent in the city policy process. This brief period of prominence offers city councilmen their best opportunity to exercise policy leadership, for at this time councilmen will be most aware of the problem's existence, and their decisions will have the most direct and immediate policy consequences. For this reason the city problems perceived by councilmen cannot be expected to predict policy outcomes closely for the total group of cities. Perceived problems may, however, be strongly related to the *dynamics* of city policy—to major changes in the level of services, to shifts in the direction of policy, or to the emergence of totally new policies.

After taking these limitations into consideration, we can still draw several conclusions about the sources of city policy problems. Zoning and planning as policy problems are both clearly related to environmental pressures generated by metropolitan expansion—actual growth in the case of planning and perceived potential change in the case of zoning. No single explanatory factor applies to amenities problems. Councilmen seem to be responding partly to needs for public amenities created by high population densities and partly to the wishes of affluent citizens who express a concern for the provision of libraries, parks, or recreational facilities in their city.

---

[5]The complex relationships among environmental pressures, problem perceptions, and city expenditures are considered in the Introduction to Part II.

Chapter 3

Taxes, Budgets, and Spending Decisions

Many possibilities for delaying, modifying, or diluting policy exist between the perception of a problem demanding city government action and the action taken in response to that problem. In using policy leadership as the explicit focus of study, we are drawn to those factors that directly limit or modify the ability of city councils to make policy decisions appropriate to their goals. Ideally, we would want to develop policy performance indicators for cities and then concentrate on those cities that have been particularly unsuccessful in reaching their goals. Unfortunately, measuring the quality of government-provided services to determine how rigorously original policy decisions are being implemented poses difficulties beyond the range of this study. In the absence of these more direct measures, we can still gain some idea of the limits imposed on the policy process simply by asking the councilmen themselves.

Some of the most important external limitations on successful policy-making are monetary. Every new program (or even the continuation of an old one requiring the expenditure of large sums of money) may or may not be undertaken depending on the availability of money and the importance city councilmen attach to the program. Councilmen must weigh new expenditures in light of both the other demands made on city government and the bare minimum of services that must be provided regardless of the availability of funds. If the tax revenue is insufficient—

or if councilmen merely *think* it insufficient—increases or innovations may be summarily ruled out of an upcoming budget.

Money, the single most important resource of city governments, operates both subjectively and objectively in determining spending decisions. One city may be compared with another according to the size of its tax base or the amount of money per capita received from other levels of government, and inferences concerning the probable willingness of the two city councils to undertake major program expansions or programs in new policy areas can be drawn from these aggregate data. The real operative variable, however, is the councilmen's actual willingness to spend. The councilmen's attitudes toward spending may be related to the objective facts of tax base or to the volume of intergovernmental grants, but these factors do not completely determine councilmen's perceptions of their city's resources. Councilmen are also involved in political relationships with each other, with the city manager, and with the citizens of their town, and council opinions probably reflect these political pressures as well as councilmen's personal feelings on governmental economy.

If councilmen do not regard these monetary and political limits as overriding constraints on their freedom to act, they will be able to exercise policy leadership in making decisions and choosing courses of action for their city. If they regard these limits as determinative, many opportunities for policy leadership will be closed to them.

Tax Base Problems

Four questions were asked of the councilmen to discover which city characteristics affect their willingness to spend the taxpayers' money. Three were open questions referring to major city problems or budgetary considerations, while the fourth was included in structured form specifically to determine how the councilmen regarded the property tax when they faced a new budget.

In response to the question dealing with pressing city problems, 44 of 433 councilmen discussed a problem relating to the city tax base.[1] Most respondents described specific substantive problems in response to this question; thus, the number of general responses relating to the tax base was very low. These 44 councilmen were concerned that the city tax base was insufficient to finance the services needed and believed that something should be done to raise the tax base. For example, one councilman said

> Industrialization of the area is a major problem. Industry is necessary to supply people with jobs and to help our tax base. Bedroom communities have all the problems of schools, recreation, services. Homes alone don't have the ability to provide all this without a fantastic property tax. Growth is tremendously fast. We try to keep the community balanced tax-wise. (Councilman 70602)

Several objective measures of the city tax base are readily available. The assessed value of real property in the city measures the base tapped by the city property tax. The percentage of the city's land area devoted to commercial and industrial uses also is commonly supposed to be a useful measure of city tax resources, because it indicates the density or concentration of taxable wealth. Commercial land uses such as shopping centers and downtown business areas are sources of sales tax revenue in addition to property tax revenue. If the city tax base is at all important in council decisions, councilmen should feel less constrained by their city's resources the higher the assessed value per capita and the higher the percentage of industrial and commercial land use.

The interview data show mixed relationships. The per capita assessed value of real property is inversely related to councilmen's perceptions of tax base problems, as shown in Table 3–1. The very low frequency of this type of problem response does not allow any firm conclusions about its relationship to actual policy decisions, however. Table 3–2, on the other hand, does not reveal any clear-cut relationship between the percentage of industrial

---

[1] The exact wording of the question was "Mr. Councilman, before talking about your work as a councilman and the work of the council itself, we would like to ask you about some of the problems facing this community. In your opinion, what are the two most pressing problems here in (city)?"

Table 3–1
Perception of Tax Base Problems,
Controlling for the Market Value of Real Property

Percentage of councilmen who mentioned an inadequate tax base as a city problem (councilmen)	*Per capita market value of real property in 1965*		
	$14,000 or more	$6,400–$13,999	Under $6400
	4 (57)	10 (285)	14 (91)

and commercial land use and the articulation of tax base problems by city councilmen.

Although an ingrained precept of local political practice is that factories and businesses represent tax windfalls for a city, some economists question their overall desirability.[2] The intensive land uses typified by commercial and industrial establishments may concentrate taxable wealth, but they also concentrate demands for public services such as police and fire protection, street maintenance, and other public utilities. Whether an additional store or factory will be a net gain or loss to a city is a complex question

Table 3–2
Perception of Tax Base Problems,
Controlling for City Land Usage

Percentage of councilmen who mentioned an inadequate tax base as a city problem (councilmen)	*Percentage of land in industrial or commercial uses in 1965*		
	20% or more	10–19%	Under 10%
	7 (100)	14 (99)	11 (140)

[2]See, for example, Julius Margolis, "Municipal Fiscal Structure in a Metropolitan Region," *Journal of Political Economy* 65 (June 1957): 225–36, and Robert C. Wood, *1400 Governments* (Cambridge, Mass.: Harvard University Press, 1961), Chapter 2.

· whose answer must depend on the type of business in question, the salary level of the required work force, and the existing services, among other things.[3] The complexity of this relationship is suggested in Table 3–2: the moderately industrial cities are those most concerned about their tax base. Highly industrial cities apparently have a sufficiently broad tax base to handle their needs, while cities with minimal levels of industrial or commercial activity apparently also have a tax base sufficient to handle their less extensive service requirements.

When city councilmen talk about their city's "tax base," they seem to mean only the property tax rolls. They do not view other forms of revenue as alternatives to the property tax but simply as supplements for it and as devices to relieve the burdens of property taxpayers:

> The property tax is a major source of revenue. We need relief in this. I would rather see money picked up with a sales tax or a use tax. The average homeowner pays $40-$50 a month in taxes, and it goes up whenever he spends money to improve his own property. That's not fair. (Councilman 60102)

> We need development of an adequate commercial center in which revenue can be obtained to alleviate the tax burden on the property owner. We have to develop some type of realistic commercial development which will produce revenues. Unless we take the burden off the homeowner, there will be chaos. Retirement people can't take it. There are many other sources that could be utilized. (Councilman 41802)

Thus, if a city depends solely on the property tax as a source of revenue, its councilmen should understandably be concerned about the tax base. Conversely, if, in addition to the property tax, the city can tap other revenue sources such as sales taxes or intergovernmental grants and rebates, councilmen should not spend nearly so much time worrying about their city's revenue base. The free responses of councilmen support this hypothesis. Table

---

[3]See Louis K. Loewenstein, "The Impact of New Industry on the Fiscal Revenues and Expenditures of Suburban Communities," *National Tax Journal* 16 (June 1963): 113–36, and Harold M. Groves and John Riew, "The Impact of Industry on Local Taxes—A Simple Model," *ibid.*, 137–45.

Table 3–3
Perception of Tax Base Problems,
Controlling for the Market Value of Real Property
and Dependence on the Property Tax

*Table entries are the percentage of councilmen in each
cell (total number shown in parentheses) who mentioned
an inadequate tax base as a city problem.*

Per capita market value of real property in 1965	Percentage of total revenue derived from the property tax in 1965		
	33% or more	25–32%	Under 25%
$14,000 or more	9 (22)	0 (16)	0 (19)
$6,400–$13,999	16 (124)	5 (93)	4 (68)
Under $6,400	36 (28)	9 (23)	5 (40)
All cities	18 (174)	5 (132)	4 (127)

3–3 shows that dependence on the property tax has a strong effect on council perceptions of tax base problems—even for cities where the size of the tax base should be sufficient to support city government expenditures.

The probable reason for Bay region councilmen's extreme sensitivity to the property tax is the *political* vulnerability of this tax as a revenue source. Many councilmen volunteered expressions of their helplessness in the face of popular low tax demands:

> One of our major budget considerations is the effect spending has on the tax rate and assessed valuation, and whether this is enough to cover particular items. The importance of an issue is not thought of as quickly as the effect it has on the tax rate. (Councilman 50301)

> We lowered taxes twice and heard nothing about it. We raised them and everybody complained. We try to maintain our present rate and won't go above it unless there is some real urgency. . . .

> We are all in agreement. We go along with new requests only if they don't raise the tax rate. (Councilman 70102)

Frequently other local service districts are responsible for the bulk of the taxpayer's property tax bill, but the city council continues to be the target of complaints—whether it consistently resists tax increases or not. Thus city governments can become scapegoats, the victims of misapprehension on the part of citizens. As one councilman remarked,

> We're down to the bone. It's difficult for the city to support itself. We may as well disincorporate and get out of the business of being a city. They want to cut $100,000 from the budget. The tax is $7.70 per $100 valuation. The city levies $.48, only 7 percent of what's levied totally. And who gets all the blasting? We get all the blasting on high taxes. (Councilman 41804)

Consequently, "low taxes" must be a part of the rhetoric of many suburban city governments regardless of councilmen's preferences.

Considering finally another presumed measure of city resources, namely, the proportion of city revenues derived from intergovernmental sources, we find in Table 3–4 that this measure is not related to councilmen's spontaneous expressions of concern about their city's tax base. This is true even for cities with very low levels of locally taxable property. Even though Bay region cities vary widely in dependence on intergovernmental sources of money, their councilmen apparently do not view these funds as aids in the solution of their own tax base problems.

An explanation for this negative finding can be found in the inflexibility of intergovernmental revenue. Rebates of this kind —gas taxes or license fees, for example—are largely determined by state formulae and are therefore fixed in absolute amount. Consequently, the more a city spends, the smaller is the percentage of city revenue deriving from intergovernmental revenue (even though the dollar amount of these funds remains constant). In other words, the intergovernmental revenue percentage reflects city expenditure policy rather than city resources. Whether or not this revenue source allows city councils to spend more on city needs, it does not seem to have any impact on councilmen's perceptions of city resource level.

Table 3–4
Perception of Tax Base Problems,
Controlling for the Market Value of Real Property
and Dependence on Intergovernmental Revenue

*Table entries are the percentage of councilmen in each
cell (total number shown in parentheses) who mentioned
an inadequate tax base as a city problem.*

Per capita market value of real property in 1965	Percentage of total revenue derived from intergovernmental sources in 1965		
	25% or more	17–24%	Under 17%
$14,000 or more	5 (19)	0 (4)	3 (34)
$6,400–$13,999	9 (64)	9 (151)	13 (75)
Under $6,400	7 (30)	15 (54)	0 (2)
All cities	8 (113)	11 (209)	10 (111)

Money and Budgetary Decisions

Two questions offered councilmen a chance to indicate that
a lack of funds limited them in making budgetary and policy
decisions. Of the 433 councilmen responding to an open question
on city problems, 117 gave answers relating to a shortage of money
for basic city services.[4] In their answers to an open question about
budgetary decisions, 158 councilmen responded that "the level of
available funds" or "the possibility of expenditure cuts" were
important in their decisions.[5] The first question identifies money

---

[4]See note 1 for the exact wording of the question.
[5]The exact wording of the question was "When the council is considering the
upcoming budget, what major considerations do you entertain about new
programs and increases?"

as a generic problem in city government; the second attempts to determine how significant actual revenues are to the expenditure decisions of city councilmen. We would expect councilmen making the responses indicated to live in cities where the local government's supply of money was somehow constricted, limited, or inflexible from year to year.

Certain aspects of governmental legal structure may also affect the level of available tax revenue. Among Bay region cities, thirty-five had statutory limits of $1 of property tax per $100 of assessed valuation, while the rest had higher limits set by their city charters. Other things being equal (e.g., popular willingness to be taxed) those cities with higher tax limits presumably would be less constricted in raising money through the property tax than those with the $1 limit. Ten Bay region cities assessed city property values themselves, while the rest used the county tax rolls as the basis for their property tax. Since the cities doing their own assessing took advantage of their autonomy to assess property at a higher percentage of market value than the prevailing county assessment ratio, we could reasonably expect that these cities would have less difficulty balancing their budget than cities relying on county assessments.

Turning first to aggregate economic measures of city resources, we find that the per capita value of real property is inversely related both to councilmen's perceptions of "paying for services" problems and to councilmen's perceptions of money as a limiting factor in budgetary decisions, as shown in Table 3-5. The latter relationship is somewhat stronger, perhaps indicating that budgetary decisions are more directly related to the city tax base than are councilmen's vague sentiments about the difficulty of paying for city services.

Surprisingly, however, neither of these council responses is related to the extent of city dependence on the property tax, as indicated by Table 3-6. Further, no pattern of relationships can be discovered when the level of per capita property value is controlled (data not shown), nor when "percentage of revenue from intergovernmental sources" is substituted for "percentage of revenue from property taxes" (data not shown). We must conclude

Table 3–5
Perception of Monetary Problems and Money
as a Budgetary Consideration,
Controlling for the Market Value of Real Property

	Per capita market value of real property in 1965		
	$14,000 or more	$6,400–$13,999	Under $6,400
Percentage of councilmen who mentioned "paying for services" as a city problem	21	28	27
(Councilmen)	(57)	(290)	(86)
Percentage of councilmen who said that "the available funds" or "cutting expenses" were important budgetary considerations	25	39	43
(Councilmen)	(52)	(279)	(81)

that council perceptions of spending limitations proceed directly
from the narrowness of the city tax base regardless of the extent
to which that tax base is actually tapped.

The two legal parameters, the $1 tax limit and the self-versus-
county assessment, display weak but consistent relationships to
councilmen's perceptions of monetary limitations, as shown in
Table 3–7. Even though all the relationships are consistent and
in the expected direction, the size of the percentage difference
is not great enough to allow us to conclude that the legal arrangements for property taxation are very important factors
in council budgetary decisions.

The Property Tax and Budgeting

Two questions in the interview schedule related directly to the
property tax as a limit on the spending desires of city councilmen.

Table 3–6
Perception of Monetary Problems and Money
as a Budgetary Consideration,
Controlling for Dependence on the Property Tax

	Percentage of total revenue derived from the property tax in 1965		
	33% or more	25–32%	Under 25%
Percentage of councilmen who mentioned "paying for services" as a city problem	25	27	28
(Councilmen)	(174)	(132)	(127)
Percentage of councilmen who said that "the available funds" or "cutting expenses" were important budgetary considerations	33	44	40
(Councilmen)	(172)	(120)	(120)

To an open question about council budgetary decisions seventy-four councilmen answered that they tried to keep the tax rate as low as possible.[6] When necessary, councilmen were then asked a closed follow-up question to determine whether the property tax was important to their budgetary decisions. In both cases, councilmen making positive responses should be found in cities where the property tax is an especially limited financing device because of either constricting legal arrangements or a narrow tax base.

Spontaneous mentions of the tax rate, summarized in Table 3–8, do not support this hypothesis. In nearly all groups of cities, irrespective of their level of expenditure or extent of dependence on the property tax, less than one councilman in five volunteered

---

[6]See note 5 for the exact wording of the question.

Table 3–7
Perception of Monetary Problems and Money
as a Budgetary Consideration,
Controlling for Legal Arrangements for Property Taxation

	Property tax limitation		Method of tax assessment	
	$1 per $100 valuation	More than $1 per $100	By county	By city
Percentage of councilmen who mentioned "paying for services" as a city problem	28	25	28	22
(Councilmen)	(240)	(193)	(373)	(60)
Percentage of councilmen who said that "the available funds" or "cutting expenses" were important budgetary considerations	41	36	40	32
(Councilmen)	(231)	(181)	(353)	(59)

a statement about the importance of the tax rate in budgetary decisions. In view of the apparently random character of these responses, we can reasonably speculate that they reflect the personal concerns of individual councilmen rather than attitudes common to all members of a city council.

Table 3–9 shows that concern for the effect of budgetary decisions on the property tax, as indicated by forced-choice responses, is strongly related to the percentage of total revenue derived from the property tax.[7] We should note, however, that the property tax is also important in budgetary decisions for many cities that do not rely heavily on this revenue source. This

---

[7]The exact wording of the question was "Does the property tax play any part in your thinking on these matters?"

Table 3–8

The Property Tax as a Budgetary Consideration,
Controlling for Total Expenditures
and Dependence on the Property Tax

*Table entries are the percentage of councilmen in each
cell (total number shown in parentheses) who mentioned
"keeping the tax rate low" as a budgetary consideration.*

Per capita expenditures in 1965	*Percentage of total revenue derived from the property tax in 1965*		
	33% or more	25–32%	Under 25%
$100 or more	19 (59)	25 (53)	14 (43)
$60–$99	25 (65)	8 (65)	25 (12)
Under $60	13 (39)	10 (10)	21 (66)
All cities	20 (163)	15 (128)	19 (121)

finding implies that minimal dependence on the property tax
actually reflects a purposely low tax policy. Since the property
tax is the most flexible revenue source on a year-to-year basis,
councilmen in cities that keep the tax rate low must especially
consider the adverse effects that budgetary increases might have
on the tax rate.

The legal arrangements for assessing property taxes should
also have some effect on the budgetary behavior of city councilmen if these arrangements impose any real limitations on city
governments. But relationships of this kind should not be taken
for granted. Analysis earlier in this chapter demonstrated that
these arrangements are not linked to the kinds of problems
councilmen perceive. Table 3–10 shows that this situation persists
when councilmen describe their budgetary deliberations. The
particular procedure chosen by a city (or chosen for it by the
terms of its charter) for assessing taxes does not produce any

Table 3–9
Importance of the Property Tax in Budgetary Decisions,
Controlling for the Market Value of Real Property
and Dependence on the Property Tax

*Table entries are the percentage of councilmen in each
cell (total number shown in parentheses) who said that the
property tax was an important factor in their budgetary
decisions.*

Per capita market value of real property in 1965	Percentage of total revenue derived from the property tax in 1965		
	33% or more	25–32%	Under 25%
$14,000 or more	86 (22)	87 (15)	27 (11)
$6,400–$13,999	90 (119)	68 (89)	54 (61)
Under $6,400	73 (26)	73 (22)	66 (47)
All cities	87 (167)	71 (126)	56 (119)

Table 3–10
Importance of the Property Tax in Budgetary Decisions,
Controlling for Legal Arrangements for Property Taxation

	Property tax limitation		Method of tax assessment	
	$1 per $100 valuation	More than $1 per $100	By county	By city
Percentage of councilmen who said that the property tax rate was an important factor in their budgetary decisions	74	71	73	69
(Councilmen)	(230)	(182)	(358)	(54)

significant council concern for the tax rate or any curtailment of the city's taxing power sufficient to affect councilmen's budgetary decisions.

Conclusions

We can draw several conclusions from this chapter. The failure to find any strong relationships between city tax laws and councilmen's perceptions suggests one possible reason why many researchers have found structural variables to be unsatisfactory predictors of policy outputs. Behaviorally, structural or legal factors presumably influence political life by affecting the actions and perceptions of political decision-makers in characteristic ways. For example, if the legal arrangements for tax assessment have any influence on the fiscal behavior of city governments, they must at some point enter the consciousness of city decision-makers to form the premises for action taken. But if tax mechanisms or other formal arrangements of government are irrelevant to decisions made by councilmen, they are probably equally irrelevant in a statistical sense to city policies. Attempting to predict policy outputs on the basis of structural factors is a futile exercise if structures are irrelevant to the political actions that produce those outputs.

On the other hand, if structural arrangements are important determinants of action and therefore of final governmental outputs, the most profitable way to study their impact on outputs is to investigate their linkage with political leaders and the decisions they make. In a sense, decision-makers intervene between governmental arrangements and political decisions. From among the many possibilities legally open to them in any particular decision, city councilmen choose one that is also personally and politically acceptable. For this reason, their attitudes may be more intimately related to the substance of policy decisions than are the structural constraints under which they operate. If this is true, informal working rules, tacit understandings, and councilmen's roles (or even prejudices) will be more significant to the policy researcher than formal mechanisms or political structure variables.

This chapter has explored only one aspect of the councilman's multifaceted involvement in the policy process, namely, his perceptions of monetary limitations on city policy. Councilmen seem to think of city finances largely in terms of the property tax. The tax rate they talk about is the property tax rate, and the tax base they worry about is the amount of wealth subject to the local property tax. They constantly look for some way to broaden the tax base and to spread the tax burden around—preferably to property owners not likely to complain about "confiscatory taxes." The availability of other revenue sources does not lessen councilmen's concern over their city's tax base, even though utilization of these sources may lower the extent of a city's actual dependence on the property tax.

These comments underline the characteristics of the property tax that have caused so much criticism and so many reform attempts. As a financing device, the property tax is too subject to assessment inequities, too visible, too politically vulnerable, and too narrow, given the size and diversity of units of local government in modern metropolitan areas.[8] The property tax is the only source of local government income that cities can increase at will; yet, for political reasons, it is highly inflexible in practice. Political necessity seems to turn some councilmen into compulsive budget cutters and tax reducers despite the objective needs of their cities or the possible decay of city services, and these attitudes are legitimized in terms of citizen desires or the will of the people. City governments are easy targets for irate citizens bent on property tax reduction even if the city itself is not responsible for the high tax rate that its citizens rebel against.

Fortunately, some city governments are able to work effectively within this framework of constraint. Part of the reason for their success may lie in the ability of city councilmen to exercise progressive leadership even in the face of monetary limitations. The variety of attitudes councilmen may take toward city development and the role of city government is the subject of the next chapter.

---

[8]These criticisms are discussed in James A. Maxwell, *Financing State and Local Governments* (Washington, D.C.: The Brookings Institution, 1965).

Chapter 4

City Policies
and Council Orientations

City Policy Development

Developmental theory normally conceives of development as a series of stages, with countries at a given stage displaying similar economic and political processes and similar governmental policy outcomes. For example, "traditional," "transitional," and "modern" are three stages that have been identified with the development of new nations. Similarly, economists have postulated a "take-off" stage for national economies.[1] But the idea of development also implies that a country must move from one stage to another, and, given the variety of factors operating in national development, this change cannot likely occur at once. More probably, a country will vacillate for a considerable period of time between two stages in such a manner that it defies classification. Yet some developmental theories exclude this possibility and base their analysis on a comparison of pure stage types.

For the purposes of this study, a more explicit treatment of policy change is desirable. Policies can be thought of as a series of policy outcomes measured on an annual basis. A "policy profile" can be defined as a small segment of this series of policy out-

---

[1]Walt W. Rostow, *The Stages of Economic Growth* (New York: Cambridge University Press, 1960).

comes, including data for several consecutive years. Several patterns may occur in this policy profile: the policy outcomes may be similar or they may differ along the dimensions used to classify them. If they are similar we can refer to them as constituting a "stage." If they differ there are again two possibilities: the outcomes may change from one stage, say stage A, to another, say stage B, without returning to the first stage, or they may fluctuate between stages A and B.

If a policy profile shows orderly movement from A to B, it should not be assigned to either stage because its policy outcomes are too dissimilar; but the regularity of change argues that this type of profile should be used in analysis. We may call this profile a "phase" of development, assuming thereby that it is produced by a governmental unit actually developing from stage A to stage B. Phases will probably be shorter in duration and less clearly bounded than stages. Operationally, stages and phases of policy development are identified solely in terms of policy outcomes, though of course the reason for making the classification is the supposed theoretical relationship between policy development and the development of popular participation or legislative institutions or a host of other politically relevant phenomena.

For each of the eighty-nine cities in this study a policy profile can be formed by plotting the amenities and planning percentage figures for the six years 1960–1965, as illustrated in Figure 4–1. These two dimensions are dichotomized at the median of the median expenditure figures for the six years—2.6% for planning expenditures and 8.55% for amenities.[2] The four cells formed by crossing these two dichotomies define four stages of policy development, and developmental phases are defined as movement between these cells.

Assuming that a policy profile can start in any one of the four quadrants and terminate in any other quadrant, there are all together twelve possible phases. To simplify the classification, however, the four hypothetical phases in which the policy profile exhibited change in both amenities and planning were not used. Of the eight remaining phases, only six contained enough cities

---

[2]Calculation of these figures is described in Appendix B, p. 168.

Figure 4–1
Examples of Policy Profiles

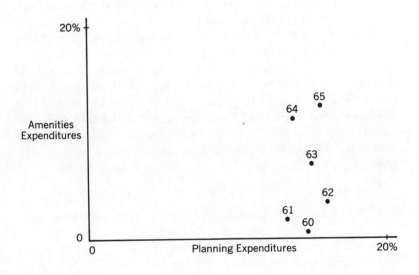

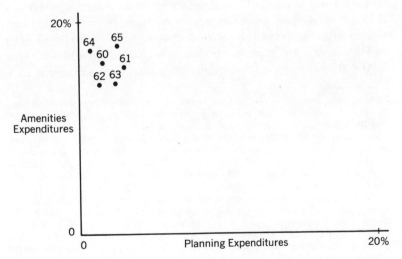

to merit separate analytic treatment. The final ten policy profile types and their designations are shown in figure 4–2.[3]

A comment should be made here about reversed development. In historical development, change is always inevitable and irreversible. Historians say that the middle ages "followed" antiquity, for example, in a way that leads one to believe that the process of change cannot be reversed. Some optimistic theories of national development also make this assumption, although in political development it can easily be shown that political decay is an everpresent possibility.[4] City policy development as discussed in this book is not assumed to be irreversible. The method of profile classification does not force any ordering on the stages of development, although theoretically we may expect that some patterns of policy change will be more common than others.

Councilmen's Change Preferences and Policies

Even if a clear causal connection between city policy outcomes and the policy preferences of city councilmen could not be established, we would still expect to find some empirical relationship between these two kinds of variables. If city councilmen merely are captives of the forces operating on their city and have no choice but to implement the policies necessitated by these forces, then surely they must come to accept these policies if they

[3]There were some deviant years in many of the eighty-nine policy profiles. In all cases assignment was made to a phase or stage according to whichever classification resulted in the smaller number of errors. Assuming the observed pattern was a stage, the number of errors would be the number of years not in the proper cell. Assuming the observed pattern to be a phase, the number of errors would be the number of years not falling into the regular pattern of change for that phase, as indicated in Figure 4–2. Thus a city with the same policy outcome in 1960 through 1964 but a different outcome in 1965 was classified as a phase city, even though there was no information available beyond 1965 to confirm or deny the assumption that city policy was actually developing. For all eighty-nine cities, the final classifications yielded sixty-one errors out of a total of 428 possible, or an error rate of 14%. The errors were distributed among all ten policy profile types with the percentage of errors ranging from 2% to 20%.
[4]Samuel P. Huntington, "Political Development and Political Decay," *World Politics* 17 (April 1965): 386–430.

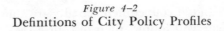

Figure 4–2
Definitions of City Policy Profiles

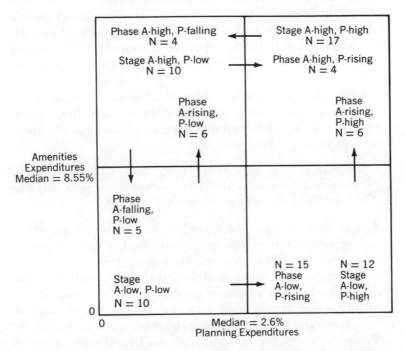

remain in office long enough. Interviews in the San Francisco Bay region indicate that councilmen actually do become reconciled to the limitations of their position as policy-makers:

> The trite answer is, I want the city just the way it was—but I realize that's not going to be. I think we should control it—have as high a standard of community life as possible. (Councilman 41201)

> What I like and what I want are two different things. I'm not sure what we can do, anyway. I do hope that we can preserve the open spaces and add to them if possible. . . . (Councilman 41305)

> I don't know what the future will be like. Cities are developed by investors. I can't project. In terms of single family units, we've gone about as far as we can. (Councilman 41505)

On the other hand, if councilmen actually are able to choose the policies their city will follow, then of course they will also indicate some preference in that direction when questioned. Councilmen may not describe reality in the terms of a political analyst, but a prediction of the general pattern of council answers should be possible once they have been coded in the terms councilmen do use.

Several questions in the interview schedule were designed to be direct measures of a councilman's policy preferences. In the main body of the interview councilmen were asked a completely open-ended question:

> Now, taking the broadest view possible, how do you see (city) in the future? I mean, what kind of a city would you personally like (city) to be in the next twenty-five years or so?

The answers received—the councilman's "future image"—were coded for favorability to change and the kind of city envisioned by the councilman (i.e., residential, balanced, or commercial). The hypothesis was that favorability to change would probably not be related to city amenities policies, but a high favorability to change would be associated with city policies designed to promote change (for example, high planning expenditures).

Table 4–1 shows the relevant data. As hypothesized, there is little relationship between amenities spending and councilmen's favorability to city change. Favorability to change is relatively high in cities where amenities expenditures are rising or high, but it is also high where amenities spending is declining. In contrast, there is a regular relationship between planning expenditures and councilmen's favorability to change. This relationship is expected because most kinds of city planning imply change, and city governments attempting to guide city change in a desired direction usually recognize the need for careful planning and anticipation of their city's probable future.

Strangely, however, councilmen in cities where planning expenditures are rising are only slightly more favorable to city change than are councilmen in cities where planning expenditures are low. If the purpose of city planning is to direct city

Table 4–1
Councilmen's Attitudes Toward City Change,
Controlling for City Expenditure Profiles

Amenities expenditures	Percentage favorable to city change*	(Councilmen)
Low	43	(137)
Falling	53	(17)
Rising	57	(42)
High	54	(144)
Planning expenditures		
Low	43	(111)
Falling	44	(25)
Rising	46	(76)
High	59	(128)
All cities	50	(340)

*The source for this attitude is described in Appendix B, p. 169.

change, we would certainly expect that councilmen in cities whose planning expenditures have been rising significantly would be favorably disposed toward change.

The explanation for this apparent discrepancy lies in the ambiguity of planning expenditures as a measure of city policy. In fact, either an active "planning" policy designed to encourage and direct change *or* a restrictive "zoning" policy designed to *prevent* change may result in a high percentage of total expenditures for planning. This is particularly true because many cities following a restrictive zoning policy maintain minimal governments and spend little beyond what is needed to provide basic city services. For these cities the planning commission expenditures constitute a large percentage of the total budget, partly because the remainder of the budget is small in absolute terms.

Councilmen in the cities in Table 4–1 whose planning expenditures are rising are generally opposed to change because most of these cities are actually following a restrictive zoning policy. These are the cities being threatened by metropolitan expansion. They have just recently increased their zoning activities (indicated here by increasing "planning" expenditures) in an effort to protect themselves, and their councilmen continue to oppose major city changes.

Since restrictive zoning cities also generally provide a minimum of services, we can test this explanation by separating cities according to the level of their amenities expenditures. Of those councilmen in cities with rising planning expenditures, only 41 percent in cities with an A-low, P-rising policy profile favor city change, while 67 percent in cities with an A-high, P-rising profile favor change. Thus, councilmen in the minimal service, restrictive zoning cities are the least favorable to city change of any group, while councilmen in high amenities, active planning cities are much more favorable to change than any other group of respondents.

Future City Images and City Policies

An examination of the goals sought by city councilmen in cities with different policy profiles will help to confirm this explanation of city policy. It is quite possible that city councils may employ similar policies in pursuit of different goals. For example, cities with rising planning expenditures could be planning for either a small residential community or a larger commercial center. The empirical connection between city expenditures and city goals is therefore important in understanding the purposes behind variant city policies.

The "future image" held by councilmen should reveal the nature of the goals toward which they are directing their city. Of course, a future image may be specific or general, remote or immediately attainable. The question asked of the councilmen did not seek to structure their answers in any way. Of the 356 codable responses, about 25 percent articulated only a very general image of the future. These men favored an appealing community with high standards of community life but they were not specific about what kind of city they had in mind. The remaining three-fourths of the councilmen placed their city on a continuum ranging from exclusively residential to predominantly industrial and commercial. In other words, 75 percent of the councilmen interviewed had developed an ideal image of their community that was expressed in terms of land use patterns. Furthermore, these councilmen took the balanced community as their reference point, deciding whether their city should deviate from that point and, if so, in which direction—more residential or more commercial development. Thus, the terms used by city decision-makers in describing their policy orientations correspond closely to the terminology used in the theory of urban policy presented in chapter 1.

Some verbal extracts can suggest more vividly the kinds of future images held by these San Francisco Bay region councilmen:

> We've got great potential. I can see getting our central business district, getting a housing project, for there's lots of poverty here, bringing men out of the fields and into work in the community. Housing standards should go up. We'll have beautification grants, a master plan. (Councilman 11302)

> I should like to see it become the space age city of the West. This city should have an identity of its own. There are many space industries here. We have a national reputation already. I'd like to see high-rises, a skyline, futuristic buildings. High-rises especially. (Councilman 32103)

> I would like to see it develop into a nice clean city—paved streets, good education facilities, and all the facilities for a happy community, and also to lower the tax rate of the city. (Councilman 41001)

> I would like to see it be a rural residential community much the way it is now. Subdivisions clustered in the lower valley and the upper areas preserved as open space. I'd like to see the streams preserved along the banks, see trails kept for people and the main thoroughfares turned into parkways. (Councilman 42503)

We cannot hypothesize about the location of "high community standards" respondents since high community standards do not by themselves imply any particular kind of city policy. On the other hand, councilmen opposed to commercial and economic development in their city should be found in cities whose policies would tend to discourage development.

Table 4-2 arranges the future images held by city councilmen according to city expenditure profiles. As expected, there is no particular relationship between amenities spending and the tendency to express specific rather than indefinite images of the city's future. Councilmen with an unspecific image of their city's future are common in cities with falling amenities expenditures, but they are equally common in cities with high amenities expenditures. Since public provision of amenities does not in itself imply any specific balance of land use in a city, it is understandable that there should be no relationship between amenities spending and the tendency to express a specific future image.

More interesting is the fact that councilmen with an unspecific future image for their city are very common in cities where amenities or planning expenditures have been falling. The implication here—necessarily speculative—is that specific future goals are necessary if city councilmen are to maintain a strong commitment to active amenities and planning policies. Councilmen without a clear image of the life style they wish to preserve may not realize the significance of amenities and planning policies and may allow expenditures in these areas to decline year by year in spite of the general upward trend of city government spending.

Although planning expenditures may be an important tool of city council policy, Table 4-2 shows that planning (or zoning) can be used to pursue a variety of goals. Of councilmen mentioning specific images, a majority in low planning cities wish their city to remain residential, but so also do a majority in cities where planning expenditures have been rising. Councilmen in high planning cities are split widely among all possible types of future images, demonstrating that the relationship between goals and expenditures is not a simple one.

One group of cities will be singled out for more detailed examination—those in which planning expenditures have increased

Table 4–2
Councilmen's Image of Their City's Future,
Controlling for City Expenditure Profiles

Amenities expenditures	Image of the city's future*				
	Residential (%)	Balanced (%)	Industrial/ Commercial (%)	Unspecific (%)	(Councilmen)
Low	49	28	6	17	(141)
Falling	34	33	0	33	(12)
Rising	33	33	17	17	(46)
High	32	27	8	33	(157)
Planning expenditures					
Low	50	23	5	22	(101)
Falling	24	28	8	40	(25)
Rising	50	26	6	18	(78)
High	27	35	11	27	(152)
All cities	38	29	8	25	(356)

*The source for this future image is described in the text.

significantly during the past six years. In discussing Table 4–1 we hypothesized that these are predominantly cities opposing change and following a restrictive zoning policy in order to remain residential. Future images held by councilmen in these cities confirm this interpretation. In the A-low, P-rising cities— those supposed to be following a restrictive zoning policy—55 percent of the councilmen favored a residential community, and 25 percent wanted a balanced or an industrial-commercial city; in the A-high, P-rising cities—those pursuing a policy of planned change—37 percent of the councilmen wanted a residential community, and 52 percent favored a balanced or an industrial-commercial city. These differences are far from complete, but they do suggest strongly that distinguishable planning and zoning policies are concealed by the planning expenditure figures in Table 4–1.

Excluding those cities following restrictive zoning policies, there seems to be no consistent relationship between future images and amenities spending. If a councilman wishes his city to be industrial or commercial, it probably already provides a high level of public amenities, according to Table 4–2; but if he wishes it to remain residential, its amenities expenditures cannot be predicted with certainty. This finding supports one part of the theory outlined in chapter 1—namely, that amenities spending may be undertaken in response to the desires of middle and upper income citizens living in residential suburbs as well as in response to the amenities needs of lower income groups living in industrial and commercial cities.

To supplement the future image question and to act as a check on it, a closed form follow-up question was asked of the councilmen. Specifically, they were asked to choose among five statements about the future role of their city government, ranging from reducing services to taking an active part in promoting city growth. These responses were used to calculate future role scores indicating how favorable various groups of councilmen were toward an active role for their city government.[5] Table 4–3 displays aggregate future role scores according to the expenditure profile for councilmen's cities.

The pattern most immediately apparent in the table is that a majority of councilmen in nearly all groups of cities favor an active governmental role. Only in cities whose planning expenditures are low or falling is this position held by a minority of councilmen. Thus, most councilmen see themselves as active leaders of their city's future development, whatever its policies. Of course, it is easy for councilmen to give this answer, since it neither commits them to anything specific nor implies any particular kinds of policy goals. As such, these responses probably tell

---

[5]Calculation of future role scores is described in Appendix B, p. 169.

Table 4–3
Councilmen's Future Role Scores,
Controlling for City Expenditure Profiles

Amenities expenditures	Aggregate future role score*	(Councilmen)
Low	1.14	(136)
Falling	1.33	(15)
Rising	1.17	(47)
High	1.22	(162)

Planning expenditures		
Low	0.95	(120)
Falling	0.96	(25)
Rising	1.32	(74)
High	1.36	(141)
All cities	1.18	(360)

*The source for this future role score is described in Appendix B, p. 169.

us more about councilmen and their perceptions of their own jobs than it reveals about city council policy leadership.

In this connection, it is particularly interesting to note the cities where planning expenditures have been rising. As a group, the councilmen in these cities are very favorable toward an active governmental role, even though these are the same men who (in Table 4–1) were strongly opposed to city change and who (in Table 4–2) strongly preferred to remain residential. Since most of these cities follow a policy of restrictive zoning to prevent change, obviously the councilmen, even if opposed to change and development, do not necessarily conceive of their job in negative terms. Councilmen apparently see "growth" as more than the simple increase of physical size or population. To them city growth may also mean steady progress toward some ideal conception of the city, or perhaps simply maintenance of the city's desirable features as it gets older and residents come and go. Thus, in many cases council policy leadership may more closely approximate the paternal image of "city father" than the aggressive and dynamic image to which the term can apply.

Table 4–3 demonstrates no relationship between amenities spending and the future role of city government as perceived by councilmen, but the data indicate that amenities spending can sometimes be related to policy leadership. The group of councilmen with the lowest aggregate future role score (0.77) are those in cities low on both amenities and planning expenditures. In contrast, councilmen in cities low on planning but high on amenities have a future role score of 1.00. Councilmen in cities low on amenities and high on planning score 1.27, while councilmen in cities high on both expenditure dimensions score 1.37.

From these figures we may conclude that either amenities or planning (or zoning) expenditures may be related to council policy leadership. There are thus at least three forms of policy leadership: the prevention of change through restrictive zoning, planned change and development, and the provision of public amenities. A need for public amenities and similar programs calls for some degree of policy leadership, but it does not require as strong a leadership orientation as the situation of rapid change and growth that produces planning or zoning policies. This finding supports the model of city policy presented in chapter 1, where we argued that imminent growth and the probability of rapid city change would provide the greatest challenge to city government policy leadership.

Budgetary Styles and Policies

There is yet another aspect of council behavior that should be related to city policy outcomes, namely, councilmen's "budgetary style." This term encompasses, among other things, the councilman's general approach to making budgetary decisions, the purposes he thinks the budget should serve, and the expenditure areas he generally favors or feels free to cut if necessary. The budget and budgetary behavior are central to the policy process because the budget (whether councilmen regard it in this light or not) presents the operational version of city policy. Because it allocates total governmental revenues among competing programs and departments, a final budget inevitably attaches priorities to these various areas of expenditure, even if councilmen insist vehemently that all city programs are equally important. In short, the budget provides an objective measure of what the councilmen find really important enough to fight for and to spend their city's tax dollars on.

Because of the importance of building several measures of budgetary behavior, the interviews with Bay region councilmen included several questions on the budget. The first question sought simply to gain an overview of the approaches to budgeting taken by city councilmen:

> When the council is considering the upcoming budget, what major considerations do you entertain about new programs and increases?

Respondents could give almost any answer to a question as broad as this, but we hoped that the kinds of answers they gave would indicate the significance they attached to the budget in the process of governing. For example, councilmen who viewed the budget as a policy instrument would probably mention a long-range capital improvement plan as one of the major factors in their decisions, while councilmen interested primarily in cutting the high cost of city government would more often mention a balanced budget as an important city goal. Thus, a councilman's budgetary style would reflect his general views on the purpose of city government, especially as they applied to the range of specific monetary decisions comprising the city budget.

Twenty distinct kinds of answers were coded from the interviews and grouped into four types of budgetary style. These types are described and illustrated below:

Programmatic: view of the budget as a planning or policy instrument

The budget is policy—I try to look at everything to see what the money is being spent for, and how it affects the city. I'm concerned about money being spent for administration versus people activities. (Councilman 31011)

We try to provide for capital improvements to support the growth that is coming. We look at the general plan and make sure we make capital improvements wisely. We have to be far-seeing. (Councilman 11405)

Rational or incremental: view of the budget as a collection of departmental services and programs

We assume that the budget we passed the previous year is a proper budget. We have examined the new programs. So through the years we pass on a number of things—what street should we improve, additional personnel. . . . I approach it on the basis of what is the difference between years on the total. Why the increase? Justify it. (Councilman 41402)

By the time we get the budget, it has been worked on by every department head. All their needs are there—it's utopia. We have to make it realistic. I think, where can we best spend the limited amount of money. I think in terms of what is most needed and desirable rather than what can we cut. This means giving priorities, so then there is an automatic cutoff. (Councilman 11602)

Formal: view of the budget as the province of the city manager

Let's face it—with a city of this size [325,000] we have to rely heavily on the manager and the professional staff to make serious recommendations. It's frightening the importance of the decisions that you have to pass over. Only 17 people were in the audience when we last passed the budget. (Councilman 32201)

We go over it and see if any increases are needed. The city manager lays it down for us. We rely heavily on him and his judgments. (Councilman 10604)

Negative: view of the budget as a list of expenses to be minimized

Fundamentally, I consider how to pay for it. If the city manager has covered this, I ask if it is necessary. I try to be economical-minded. I want no frills. (Councilman 11403)

First, that the property tax is not increased. This is an overwhelming political fact of life here. Within this restriction, we should obtain a maximum amount of services. (Councilman 21304)

Councilmen whose approach to budgeting allows them great flexibility in allocating money to various programs should more likely be found in cities undergoing policy change than in stable cities. Councilmen whose budget decisions are locked into past choices either by a personal preference for gradualism or by monetary limitations—low revenues or citizen demands for low taxes, for example—should be found more often in stable cities than in cities undergoing policy change, and more often in low spending cities than in high spending cities. In short, for a city government to alter or reverse its policy outputs it must be able to budget these changes from year to year relatively unhampered by past decisions or "normal" levels of allocation for its various programs.

If the rational-incremental budgetary style is thought of as the standard or customary approach to budgeting, the other styles may be said to represent deviations from it. A negative budgetary style implies strict limits on city spending of any kind; hence councilmen using this style should be found in low spending cities. Programmatic budgeting implies that policy decisions may be directly implemented in the budget without regard to previous or expected levels of spending; hence programmatic councilmen should be found in cities where expenditures are changing more frequently than in cities where spending levels are remaining stationary. A formal approach to the budget implies considerable reliance on the city manager and the requests he makes on behalf of the city departments. In view of the increasing professionalization of city managers, councilmen deferring to the manager would likely be found in cities with high levels of planning activity, but reliance on the city manager does not imply anything more specific about city policies.

Table 4–4 shows that negative budgetary styles are widely distributed according to city expenditure profiles. Councilmen taking this approach to a budget are less common in cities with rising or high levels of amenities expenditures, but they are found with roughly equal frequency at all levels of planning expenditures. A possible explanation for this pattern is that cities arrive at their present level of planning expenditures in response to forces other than the budgetary styles of their councilmen. If the need for a new planning or zoning policy becomes particularly acute at a particular period of a city's development, as hypothesized in chapter 1, then this need will probably override the normal budgetary rules that councilmen have adopted. But since the need for public amenities is never as imperative or as sudden as the need for planning or zoning, standing budgetary styles will be more clearly reflected in amenities than in planning expenditures.

The restrictive zoning cities illustrate this conjectural explanation. A total of 43 percent of the budgetary style responses in these cities were negative. Councils in these cities have been forced to increase their planning activities to prevent change from occurring, but since they still favor minimal services and low taxes their councilmen adhere to a negative budgetary style despite the expenditures they are forced to make by outside circumstances.

Formal budgetary styles are found, as predicted, everywhere except in cities with consistently low planning expenditures, but the low frequency of this response casts serious doubt on its significance in city budgetary decisions. Very few councilmen—primarily those in large cities—were willing to admit that they relied on the city manager as a policy leader.

Surprisingly, programmatic budgetary styles are not related to planning expenditures, as we would expect if city planning were being used to estimate future service needs and to plan bond issues and capital purchases. The data in Table 4–4 also do not support the hypothesis that a programmatic style will be more common in cities undergoing policy change than in other cities. On the other hand, programmatic councilmen are more common in cities with rising or high levels of amenities spending than in other cities.

The explanation for these relationships may again lie in the difference between the needs for public amenities spending and the needs for planning or zoning activity. A broader scope of city government activity (indicated here by increasing amenities expenditures) may require or call forth a more programmatic orientation to budgetary decisions. Since the needs for public amenities are not usually crucial or sudden, increases in amenities programs can be made over a period of years in accordance with a long-range plan of some kind. In the case of planning or zoning

Table 4–4
Councilmen's Budgetary Styles,
Controlling for City Expenditure Profiles

Amenities expenditures	Councilmen's budgetary styles*				
	Programmatic (%)	Rational (%)	Formal (%)	Negative (%)	(Total mentions)
Low	11	33	10	46	(233)
Falling	11	45	0	44	(27)
Rising	14	49	8	29	(92)
High	19	36	10	35	(303)
Planning expenditures					
Low	14	43	5	38	(190)
Falling	27	27	17	29	(48)
Rising	14	34	12	40	(145)
High	15	36	10	39	(272)
All cities	15	38	9	38	(655)

*The source for these budgetary styles is described in the text.

expenditures, however, the need for policy change arises more suddenly, and decisions must be made more rapidly if they are to be effective in dealing with the problems posed by imminent city change. Consequently, planning or zoning expenditure decisions cannot be made according to a set program—even though the planning expenditures themselves may result in the establishment of such a program. Only after immediate pressures have been relieved will councilmen be free to make expenditure decisions according to some standing procedure.

The nature of the budgetary style responses presented in Table 4–4 underlines the flexibility in budgetary decision-making. Many councilmen gave responses fitting into several categories. For example, a negative style was frequently combined with a rational or programmatic style. Thus, city councilmen could make decisions according to a programmatic framework when they had the opportunity, negatively when there were no pressing needs, and rationally otherwise. If this is the usual practice, the "normal" budgetary procedures followed by a city council will be largely irrelevant to its exercise of policy leadership. The opportunities for policy leadership and the pressures for major policy change—at least for planning and zoning policies—require that major policy decisions be made largely outside the incremental framework of the budgetary process.[6]

Budget Cutting and City Policies

Since budgetary styles apparently reflect "normal" modes of council operation, they do not tell us how city councilmen will react to unusual demands and pressures; an examination of councilmen's commitments to various kinds of governmental programs, however, may help us to predict their reaction. Bay region councilmen were asked the following question:

> Let's suppose that the people in this city were all agreed that the city budget and local taxes *both* had to be reduced. Would you have any preferences as to what services should be cut and what ones should not be cut?

This hypothetical question (for some respondents it was very realistic) forced councilmen to demonstrate in a concrete way their commitment—or lack of it—to the various functions of city government. If a councilman preferred to preserve amenities programs, for example, when he was under popular pressure to cut expenditures, we could infer that he strongly favored publicly provided amenities in his city. Similarly, the first program he

---

[6]This conclusion is implicit in the work of Davis, Dempster, and Wildavsky on federal budgeting, in which they find that major policy changes cannot be explained by the standard rules of budgetary strategy. See Otto A. Davis, M.A.H. Dempster, and Aaron Wildavsky, "A Theory of the Budgetary Process," *American Political Science Review* 60 (September 1966): 529–47.

would cut must be one that he already thought was only marginally useful.

Table 4–5 summarizes some of the answers to this question. The import of this table is quite clear: the greater the level of expenditures in a particular category, the more willing councilmen will be to cut that category if necessary. From these figures we can also conclude that many amenities and planning spending decisions must be made outside the normal procedures for city budgeting, because if they were subject to the usual budgetary procedures there would be little reason to budget anything at all for these purposes. Any attempt to increase amenities or planning allocations would be met by a tendency to cut them back again.

These conclusions are supported by councilmen's indications respecting which programs should not be cut, shown in Table 4–6. Very few councilmen express a commitment to amenities or planning as valuable city programs. Instead, the majority mention the basic, essential city services such as fire and police protection, sewerage and drainage facilities, water supply, and other publicly owned utilities. Most councilmen apparently view these services as the core of the city budget—something that should not be cut back until all other programs have been pared as much as possible. The second most common answer is simply that it is impossible to cut anything: expenditures are already so low that there is nothing in the budget that is not absolutely necessary.

As Table 4–6 shows, councilmen tend not to single out basic city services for protection until they have discovered other areas where they can cut the budget: councilmen in cities low on both amenities and planning cannot find anything to cut back. The more programs a city government undertakes, the easier its councilmen will be able to identify and agree on the essential and expendable items in a budget.

In summary, the approach city councilmen take to the task of budgeting appears to be largely determined by the number and size of the programs about which they are making decisions rather than the policy significance of any particular kind of expenditure. In the face of popular demands to limit spending,

Table 4–5
Councilmen's Budget Cutting Preferences,
for Selected Groups of Cities

| | *Area of the budget that can be cut** | | | | |
Expenditure profile	Services (%)	Amenities (%)	Outlays, planning (%)	Across board, can't cut specific area (%)	(Total mentions)
Low on both amenities and planning	24	14	8	54	(37)
High on both amenities and planning	24	36	17	23	(115)
All cities	26	32	16	26	(483)

*The source for these preferences is described in the text.

councilmen will defend the basic city services or, if these are already minimal, deny the possibility of any budget cuts. Basic program and policy decisions apparently are made quite independently of routine budgetary decisions and according to different rules. The kinds of data available through interview techniques are unfortunately inadequate to reveal the relationship between these policy decisions and their implementation in the city budget.

Conclusions

The relationship between the policy preferences of city councilmen and the policies of their governments is not simple. The degree to which a councilman favors city change is related to the position of his city in a developmental sequence. Regardless of how a councilman views city change, however, he will have a de-

Table 4–6
Councilmen's Budget Cutting Preferences,
for Selected Groups of Cities, *continued*

Expenditure profile	*Area of the budget that should not be cut**				
	Services (%)	Amenities (%)	Outlays, planning (%)	Across board, can't cut specific area (%)	(Total mentions)
Low on both amenities and planning	34	0	0	66	(29)
High on both amenities and planning	55	11	0	34	(83)
All cities	55	8	2	35	(367)

*The source for these preferences is described in the text.

finite idea of the kind of city he would like to live in, an image articulated in terms of a balance of types of land use—residential, commercial, or industrial. Cities following similar policies may be aiming at different policy goals, and the same goal may be approached through a variety of city policy mixtures. In nearly all cases, however, planning expenditures are strongly related to the desire for a more active city government, a broader scope of city government activity, and some kind of change in city character. The only exception to this generalization is the group of cities in which planning expenditures represent an attempt to impose restrictive zoning ordinances in order to prevent development. Councilmen in these cities oppose change but nonetheless conceive of themselves as taking an active part in their city's future.

The approach a councilman takes to budgeting is loosely related to his orientation to city change, but his budgetary style seems to be determined as much by the pattern of his city's policy as the reverse. The presence or absence of certain programs allows councilmen a greater or lesser degree of freedom when they attempt to fit a variety of city programs into a limited budget. When pressed, nearly all councilmen could cut their budget somewhere, but where they cut it depends to a great extent on what is actually in the budget. Faced with the necessity of cutting the budget, some councilmen will remove what appear to them to be frills, regardless of the long-term effects or policy consequences these cuts may have. Many others, however, insist that there is nothing they can delete or say that they would prefer to cut across the board rather than single out any one program. In addition, nearly all councilmen will stop short of cutting back on basic city utilities and protection services.

Policy leadership is weakly related to council budgetary styles. Many city councilmen favorable to city change and to an active role for city government nevertheless approach a budget hoping to cut expenditures wherever possible. Two budgetary styles—the formal and the programmatic—are logically related to policy leadership, but they do not occur frequently. Apparently both the city council and the city manager can use the budget as an instrument of policy leadership, but very few councilmen are willing to admit that they rely on the city manager for policy decisions.

The fact that a majority of cities following active policies are governed by city councils using conservative budgetary techniques strongly suggests that many of the important policy decisions made in city government are not made in the context of the city's annual budget. Apparently many city councils exercise policy leadership, as the term is defined in this study, even in the face of serious spending limitations. Council commitment to policies and city goals is examined in Part II in the context of constraints on the policy process exerted by outside forces such as available resources and the desires of citizens.

Part II

The Councils
and Their Policies

Part I of this study used the individual city councilman as the unit of analysis. Chapters 2, 3, and 4 explored the relationship between the councilman and his city—his problems, his constraints, and his preferences. No assumptions were made about the direction of causality between the variables being crosstabulated, although some causal interpretations were suggested. In Part II the viewpoint of data analysis will be reversed. City councilmen will be considered as independent, purposive actors rather than as recipients of environmental pressures and forces. The feelings expressed by individual councilmen will be combined so that statements can be made about councils as decision units.

In chapter 5 the variables related to city policy development are assumed to be independent of each other, and multiple regression is used to determine which factors are most important as predictors of city policy development. In chapter 6 these same variables are assumed to be causally interrelated, and causal models are constructed to determine how much independent influence city councils have in the policy process.

Individual and Aggregate Analysis

Several methodological questions must be treated before proceeding with a causal analysis of the city policy process. The first question concerns the formation of aggregate measures. Although the interview data reported in this study were gathered through interviews with individual councilmen, the data will be reported at the council level in chapters 5, 6, and 7. The justification for treating the data in this manner follows directly from the analytic focus of this study. Policy leadership, as defined in this book, is an emerging characteristic properly belonging to each city council as a whole rather than to any of its individual members. The policy decisions that provide concrete evidence of policy leadership are always collective decisions and must be agreed to by at least a majority of council members. Yet, a methodological difficulty arises in trying to form appropriate council-level measures from individual data.

Fortunately, this theoretical problem can be bypassed to some extent because of the unusual character of interview data. The problems an individual councilman perceives and the attitudes he expresses in an interview situation do not necessarily represent his own feelings divorced from any influence of his colleagues. In fact, expressed attitudes and perceptions are as much a product of council policy deliberations as are policy decisions themselves. At the time of interviewing, most councils had made a number of important policy decisions as a group—annual budget allocations, for example—that usually produced a definite convergence of councilmen's opinions. Consequently, the attitudes and perceptions revealed by interviews with individual councilmen are not tied to any particular decision, but reflect more general predispositions.

If this is true, then interviews with individual councilmen tap a prevailing set of council attitudes. To a large extent the analytic macro-micro gap is already bridged by the respondents themselves. The combined results from interviews with members of the same council can be treated as a measure of a *council* attitude or preference. For example, a council in which only one member mentioned planning as a city problem would be less concerned about planning policies than a council in which three members mentioned planning as a problem.

The only remaining step in linking the attitudes of city councilmen to actual expenditures is that of translating council attitudes into expenditure decisions. The obvious assumption to make is that attitudes will be translated into expenditures in direct proportion to their intensity. Thus, if council attitudes are the primary influence on planning expenditures, a council twice as concerned about planning as another council would be expected to spend twice as much for planning.

This assumption is made because it is simple and because we do not know the details of decision-making in individual councils; but it is also plausible. Most decisions are not simple "yes" or "no" choices, but, rather, offer some latitude for compromise. Differences between individual councilmen can usually be worked out through a form of compromise, especially in spending decisions. Thus, a strong and unified council attitude will be translated into a high level of expenditures, while a weak or divided council attitude will be translated into a lower level of expenditures.

Chapter 5 presents the results of council-level analysis for Bay region cities. In general, the councilmen actually interviewed from a given city are assumed to provide the best sample of the attitudes and perceptions of the whole council. For any individual measure, however, a council is not included in the analysis unless codable responses were received from a majority of its members. Leaving out the cities in which a majority of councilmen were never contacted, the maximum usable sample becomes eighty-four cities of a possible eighty-nine, based on 428 individual interviews of a possible 488.

Correlations and Causal Inferences

The second methodological problem that must be considered is the technique of causal analysis once appropriate council measures have been constructed. Here we may usefully distinguish among several possible situations. The policy process respecting a specific category of expenditures has three distinct states: a city may never have spent much money in this category, may now be spending a large amount in the category, or may be in a state of transition between high and low spending. The first two states are symptomatic of equilibrium in the policy process. For cities in these circumstances policy maintains a desired equilibrium in the face of influences from outside.

For example, if outside land developers threaten to subdivide a high income residential suburb, a restrictive city zoning policy may prevent subdivision from occurring. Here city policy maintains equilibrium by opposing exogenous changes. In another city threatened by development a city planning policy may be formulated that directs city growth. In this case an equilibrium condition of planned change may be reached. These two types of equilibrium are diagrammed in Figure II–1. They would continue to exist until some exogenous change occurred, such as a decline in the pressures for development, the election of councilmen with different preferences, or the appointment of a new city manager who implemented policy decisions differently from his predecessor.

For cities in an equilibrium state it is impossible to discover unidirectional causal linkages between variables because, in fact, reciprocal causation is operating. Each variable reinforces the others. The direction of causality between any two variables is most clearly revealed when policy is in a state of transition. Consequently, it is desirable to isolate, if only roughly, those few cities in the process of policy change. The reason for isolating these cities can be explained more clearly by referring to the three policy process states just mentioned.

For example, in low amenities cities the councils will be concerned about neither amenities problems nor citizen desires for amenities programs. Hence, the correlation between amenities spending and council concern for amenities in this group of cities may be either positive or negative, but it will probably be low and statistically insignificant. Normally, in a cycle of policy formation we would expect first the generation of greater needs or desires for amenities, then the city council's recognition of this situation, and finally its development of programs to meet the needs perceived. When councilmen first recognize new amenities needs, the relationship between their perceptions and their city's policy will be strongly negative since expenditures have not yet been increased to meet the greater need. While councils are formulating and implementing new programs, the

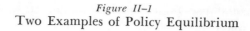

Figure II–1
Two Examples of Policy Equilibrium

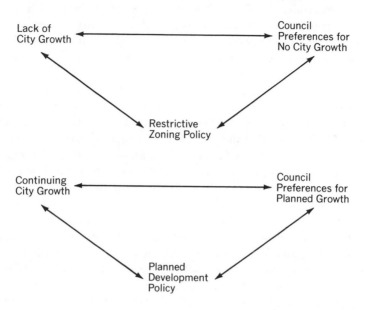

relationship between perceived amenities needs and actual amenities expenditures should be positive because the initial council concern for amenities has not declined. In the third state of the policy process, when new programs have been in operation for some time, the level of amenities expenditures should be negatively related to a concern for amenities because the new programs will begin to fill the perceived amenities needs and to remove amenities from the immediate attention of the city council.

The obvious reason for trying to separate cities at different states in the policy cycle is that otherwise it will be difficult to interpret a correlation between council problem perceptions and actual city expenditures. If the correlation between perception of amenities problems and amenities expenditures for the entire population of cities is not significant, for example, we cannot be sure whether the population contains mostly cities in the early stages of the policy process, a mixture of middle and late stage cities, or whether, in fact, there is no relationship between perceptions and expenditures. If we cannot be certain about the size and direction of the various correlations involved, we cannot speculate about the nature of underlying causal linkages. If cities in different stages of the policy process can be separated even roughly, however, we can attempt causal analysis.

For cities undergoing policy change, several kinds of causal sequences may be found. For example, the effects of metropolitan expansion may change a city's environmental character first—the growth rate may accelerate—or they may influence the city council first—it may become more favorable toward city planning. A

Figure II–2
Three Possibilities for Policy Change

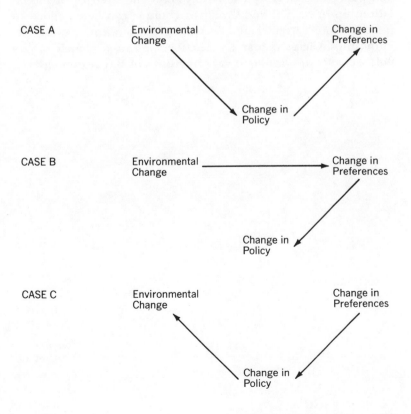

change in the city growth rate may first stimulate a change in city policy and then a change in city council preferences, or it may cause preferences to change, in turn producing a change in city policies. These three simplified possibilities are shown in Figure II–2.

If there are enough cities where the policy process is in flux, it should be possible to determine which of these three models fits the data closest by mathematically partialling out the effect of one of the variables. For example, controlling for environmental characteristics in Figure II–2 would lower the strength of the relationship between policy and preferences in cases A and B but not in case C. Controlling for preferences would have no effect on the relationship between environmental characteristics and policy in case A, but it would lower the strength of the relationship in cases B and C. This technique can be extended to include more variables and increasingly complicated causal relationships. Chapters 6 and 7 describe the causal models of city policy change applicable to various groups of Bay region cities.

Chapter 5

Policy Development and the Policy Process

The last three chapters have explored three aspects of the city policy process: problems and challenges to city policy, limitations on city programs imposed by the level of available resources, and policies themselves as they relate to the preferences of councilmen. Relatively simple relationships were investigated using simple methods of data analysis. The next two chapters attempt to bring together the separate relationships already demonstrated in order to weigh their relative importance. Many factors are related to policy change, but some are probably more closely related than others. In addition, some factors may cause policy change, while others may merely accompany it. By viewing the above relationships together, we may be able to determine which ones are critical for city policy development.

Types of City Policy

Although the theory of city policy development presented in chapter 1 did not specify whether the terminal developmental stage involved a high or a low level of planning expenditures, chapters 2, 3, and 4 did suggest some relevant conclusions. Few of the older, larger, more diversified cities in the Bay region find themselves in such a favorable position that they can do without planning commitments, either for capital purchase scheduling or for urban redevelopment. Nearly all these cities also provide extensive public amenities. Furthermore, increases in either planning or amenities expenditures seem to be related to active council leadership.

These characteristics of city policy outputs allow us to construct an empirical sequence of policy development, operationally defined as follows:

> RETARDED stage—expenditure profiles low on both amenities and planning
>
> EMERGENT phase—expenditure profiles low on one dimension and rising or falling on the other
>
> TRANSITIONAL stage—expenditure profiles low on one dimension and high on the other
>
> MATURING phase—expenditure profiles high on one dimension and rising or falling on the other
>
> ADVANCED stage—expenditure profiles high on both amenities and planning

These types are simply combinations of the policy profiles defined in chapter 4. Names are supplied only for convenience and do not imply any normative judgment about the position of a city in the typology.

This typology is not just another way of summarizing the total expenditures of a city government, as shown by Table 5–1. Since the proportion of a city budget devoted to amenities and planning rarely exceeds one-fourth, the total expenditure level is more directly determined by basic service needs than by "optional" forms of expenditure like amenities and planning. The expenditure of large sums does not guarantee that a city will get a high score on this typology of policy development.

Before attempting to weigh the relative significance of the various factors that might account for policy development, we should examine separately the relationship between policy development and the supposed causal variables to see how regular these relationships are. There is no reason to suppose that the developmental typology will necessarily be related to any other variable in a linear or even monotonic fashion, and correctly interpreting the predictive power of various supposed causes of

Table 5-1
Policy Measures and City Policy Development

| Measure of city policy | Position in development typology | | | | |
	Retarded (N = 10)	Emergent (N = 26)	Transi-tional (N = 22)	Maturing (N = 14)	Advanced (N = 17)
Median value, per capita expenditures, fiscal 1965	$95.27	$81.74	$62.14	$101.66	$95.93
Median value, amenities expenditures as a percentage of all expenditures, fiscal 1965	1.8%	6.2%	8.8%	13.4%	15.7%
Median value, planning expenditures as a percentage of general governmental expenditures, fiscal 1965	0.3%	3.4%	3.8%	3.2%	5.5%
Median value, tax rate in dollars per hundred, fiscal 1965	$1.06	$1.31	$1.41	$1.27	$1.40

policy development will be very difficult unless the peculiar characteristics of the individual relationships are known.

Policy Development and Environmental Pressures

The development typology is strongly related to environmental pressures for policy change, as shown in Table 5–2, but the relationships are not completely regular. Population density is directly related to a city's position in the typology, but rate of population increase declines for Advanced cities. The fact that this dip in growth rate is not reflected in a decline of planning expenditures (see Table 5-1) indicates that cities with Advanced policies find reasons other than growth for continuing to spend money for city planning. Another set of pressures may account for the persistence of high planning expenditures, or policy leadership may be particularly important in these cities.

In any case, Table 5-2 clearly demonstrates that a city's ecological and policy development proceed together. The more developed a city's policy is, the more likely the city is to be densely settled, to be in the older core areas of the region (as shown by the urban realm typology), and to have a substantial industrial and commercial section. These relationships are not complete, but they do appear strongly in the data.

The deviant cases merit a brief investigation. As Table 5-2 indicates, an Advanced policy may be undertaken by cities not in the traditional core areas of an urban region. Among the seventeen cities in the Bay region with Advanced policy profiles, four were located in outlying areas of the region. Of these, three were over 2000 persons per square mile in density and one was over 4000. Three of these cities were actually outlying centers of commerce within the region and hence could not be described adequately by their urban realm designation alone. These deviant cases suggest that the notion of urban realms may be too broad to pinpoint all highly developed cities. City development and attendant policy development may occur at different rates within a given realm owing to pressures that are limited to specific cities rather than characteristic of the realm as a whole.

Policy Development and Council Problem Perceptions

Changes in a city's ecological character like increased population or higher density are linked to the city policy process in several ways. One of these linkages is through the problems perceived by city decision-makers. City councils deal with a wide range of city problems; hence, they see no single problem as

Table 5–2
Environmental Variables and City Policy Development*

Environmental variable	Position in development typology				
	Retarded (N=10)	Emergent (N=26)	Transi-tional (N=22)	Maturing (N=14)	Advanced (N=17)
Median value, density in persons per square mile, 1965	1090	1950	2518	2920	3124
Median value, population increase, 1960–1965	1.4%	14.8%	18.2%	34.4%	21.4%
Median value, industrial and commercial land use, 1965	4%	8%	7%	16%	13%
Urban realms:					
Core, prairie residential, and noncentric industrial areas	10%	31%	23%	50%	41%
Railroad suburbs, noncentric residential areas	30	34	54	43	35
Urbanizing and nonmetro areas	60	35	23	7	24
	100%	100%	100%	100%	100%

*Excludes one city incorporated in 1965.

overwhelmingly important. The two areas concentrated on in this study, amenities and planning, account for less than half the important city problems perceived by Bay region councils. As a city's ecological and policy development proceed, new problems displace older ones in the minds of city decision-makers. City problems do not disappear simply because city governments pursue "advanced" policies. The reverse is more nearly true: "no problems" was one of the two most frequent problem responses in two Retarded cities, two Emergent cities, and three Transitional cities but was never mentioned in Maturing cities and was mentioned in only one Advanced city. Instead of looking at the number of problems a city has, then, we should examine the kinds of problems perceived by councils in cities at various stages of policy development.

Table 5-3 attests that the relationship between problem perceptions and policy outputs is not simple. Perception of amenities problems, for example, is related to amenities spending in a manner that is understandable but not readily susceptible to statistical representation: amenities problems are mentioned most frequently when a city is beginning to increase its amenities expenditures—presumably at the time when the disparity between amenities needs and amenities programs is greatest. In Retarded cities amenities are not a problem because there is little demand for such programs; in more developed cities amenities are not a problem because the need has been substantially met or because more important problems demand the councilmen's attention. Thus, the character of the amenities relationship is neither linear nor monotonic but more nearly resembles an "impulse" received by political decision-makers in the middle of a sequence of policy development.

Second, city councils do not appear to worry about planning and zoning programs in the abstract. As city policy develops and specific programs in these areas come into operation, councils become less concerned about the programs *per se*. Instead, they express concern about the concrete results of these programs, such as attracting business and industry to the city, promoting urban renewal, bolstering the city tax base, or improving the city image. In Table 5-3 this change occurs between the Emergent phase and the Transitional stage of policy development.

As greater city diversity raises increasingly varied problems for city governments, councils tend to view planning and zoning policies as means to desired substantive goals rather than as ends in themselves. Thus, a linkage between decision-makers and their

Table 5–3
City Problems and City Policy Development

Two most frequently mentioned problems	Position in development typology				
	Retarded (N = 9)	Emergent (N = 21)	Transitional (N = 20)	Maturing (N = 14)	Advanced (N = 17)
Basic services	30%	15%	14%	15%	6%
Planning, zoning	32	23	18	17	18
Amenities	0	15	4	5	6
Governmental and intergovernmental	19	10	8	19	15
Streets, urban renewal, industrial or commercial development	13	18	44	24	34
Paying for services	0	12	8	14	6
Social	6	7	4	6	15
	100%	100%	100%	100%	100%
(Council responses)	(18)	(42)	(39)	(28)	(33)

environment, while important at all levels of policy development (indicated here by the sum of planning, zoning, and redevelopment problem responses), may take a different form as policy changes from one stage to another. Here, again, is an important linkage in the policy process that cannot easily be handled by statistical methods. We might expect that council policy leadership would display a similar pattern—being particularly important only at certain stages in policy development. If so, assessing the importance of policy leadership may be a more complex and difficult task than is commonly supposed.

Policy Outcomes and City Resources

One important factor that may enhance or limit the ability of city councils to exercise policy leadership is the level of resources available to the city. Table 5–4 shows some of the resource measures that have already been used in chapter 3. Neither the per capita assessed value of real property nor the extent of dependence on the property tax is related to city policy development. One obvious reason why the property tax does not seriously hinder policy development, despite the high level of council concern about property tax rates, is that Advanced policies do not require a greater dollar volume of expenditures than Retarded policies.

A second reason why the property tax base of a city does not limit its policy development is that diversified industrial and commercial cities do not reap much benefit from their diversity. Table 5–4 shows that these cities do not have a higher assessed valuation even though they do have a higher proportion of supposedly desirable types of land use. The explanation, of course, is that the residential property in older industrial and commercial centers is less valuable than the residential property in suburbs without substantial concentrations of industry.

The legal arrangements for city property taxation may be important determinants of a city's resource level even though they are not, according to chapter 3, direct influences on council budgetary or tax decisions. Cities can be limited to a basic property tax rate of $1 per $100 of assessed valuation, or they can be free to levy a higher tax rate. Cities can assess property themselves, or they can let the county do it; if they do their own assessing, they can assess at a higher percentage of real value than the county does.[1] In both cases greater city freedom to tax should be related to greater policy development.

According to Table 5–4, a city cannot follow either a Maturing or an Advanced policy unless it has somehow acquired a high tax limit. Self-assessment is apparently not necessary for advanced policy, but cities that are self-assessing are more likely to have

---

[1]Since 1965, differential assessment practices have been made illegal in California. All city and county assessors are now required to assess property at 25% of market value. At the time of interviewing, this ratio ranged between 19.3% and 43.6% for Bay region cities. The number of deviant cities was not great, however: the correlation between market and assessed value for all Bay region cities was greater than +.90.

Table 5–4
Resource Measures and City Policy Development

Resource measure	*Position in development typology*				
	Retarded	Emergent	Transi-tional	Maturing	Advanced
Median value, assessed value of real property per capita, 1965	$2438	$2286	$1807	$2300	$2477
Median value, percentage of revenue from property tax, fiscal 1965	30.9%	28.7%	34.9%	31.2%	31.7%
Statutory tax limit more than $1 per $100	10%	23%	27%	64%	76%
Property assessment by self (Cities)	0% (10)	4% (26)	9% (22)	14% (14)	29% (17)
Property tax *not* an important consideration in budgeting (Councils)	22% (9)	18% (22)	19% (21)	43% (14)	29% (17)

Advanced policies than cities that are not. These relationships may be partly spurious, however, because a high tax limit and self-assessment are found more often in older, larger cities than in more recently incorporated smaller cities. Since older and larger cities are more often densely settled and industrial or commercial than younger and smaller cities, these tax structure variables may be partially a measure of city age and environmental pressures for amenities and planning expenditures.

Council attitudes toward the property tax, a final measure

related to city resources, are largely subjective rather than objective. They apparently measure a separate aspect of city resources because, as Table 5–4 shows, their relationship to city policy development is quite different from that between policy development and objective resource measures. Although a majority of city councils, regardless of policy type, worry about the effects of spending on the tax rate, this concern is less prevalent in Maturing and Advanced cities than elsewhere.

This relationship may reflect an independent change of attitude for councils in cities with advanced policies, but it may also reflect the greater tax freedom in these cities. To be specific, a majority of cities with Maturing and Advanced policies have a tax limit over $1 per $100, but a majority of all other cities have a lower tax limit.[2] Here is an opportunity for council policy leadership. If council attitudes simply reflect structural arrangements and legal constraints, then city councils have little freedom of action and can exercise little policy leadership. If these constraints do not exist, however, city councils will be in a position to exercise policy leadership. Later causal analysis will reveal whether councils actually take advantage of this opportunity.

In any case, we can tentatively conclude that the level of resources available to a city government will be linked to city governmental policies both directly through actual limitations on spending and indirectly through council perceptions of the importance of resources. These linkages may reinforce each other, but they may also work in opposing directions.

Policy Outcomes and Citizen Desires

Legislative bodies like city councils are customarily regarded as representational devices designed to express and implement the wishes of various constituencies. In discussing policy leadership, however, we may more usefully think of citizen desires as forming a constraining context within which policy leadership

---

[2]The property tax rate is higher than $1 per $100 valuation in some cities with $1 limits because tax overrides can be voted by city referendum for specified purposes (California Statutes, section 43068).

may or may not be exercised. In this view, citizen conflicts over questions of public policy indicate the importance of citizen support at various stages of policy development.

Table 5–5 presents some evidence relating citizen desires to city policy, as these relationships are perceived by city councils. Councilmen were asked to rank the importance of a number of conflicts in their city. Three of these conflicts were related to city policy development and the remainder were not.[3] The high rankings given to the three policy-relevant conflicts, as shown in Table 5–5, indicate that citizen conflicts are obviously important in Bay region cities. City planning decisions, for instance, are always made in an atmosphere of conflict, as the councilmen see it. This is quite understandable in terms of the theory presented in chapter 1, since planning decisions are closely related to the city life styles that are the primary focus of city politics. Even though planning conflicts are most important in Emerging cities, where planning expenditures are just beginning to rise, they do not seem to prevent city policy development since they do not decline in importance even in cities following Advanced policies.

The basic conflict brought about by city growth—that between old and new residents—declines in significance in Advanced cities, reflecting the fact that the rate of growth in these cities is also falling.

Conflicts over city tax policy are also important in all groups of cities, but they are somewhat less important in Maturing cities than elsewhere. In fact, tax conflicts, statutory tax limits, and council perceptions of the importance of the property tax are all related. In Maturing and Advanced cities the tax rate limit is higher, councils are less concerned about the effect of spending on the tax rate, and—for some cities—tax decisions are less controversial than in Retarded, Emergent, and Transitional cities. Somehow, then, several cities at the higher levels of policy development have managed to escape the constraints of the "low tax ideology" prevailing elsewhere. Other cities, however, follow Advanced policies even in the face of popular conflict over tax

---

[3]Specific conflicts and the coding rules for individual councils are described in Appendix B, p. 172.

Table 5–5
Citizen Desires and City Policy Development

| Measure of citizen desires | Position in development typology | | | | |
	Retarded	Emergent	Transi-tional	Maturing	Advanced
Median ranking of citizen conflicts (out of 9):					
Old vs. new residents	2.5	3.0	2.5	2.5	4.0
(Councils)	(6)	(17)	(16)	(10)	(12)
Supporters of planning vs. opponents	2.0	1.0	2.0	2.0	2.0
(Councils)	(7)	(18)	(19)	(11)	(13)
Supporters of new taxes vs. opponents	3.0	3.0	3.0	4.0	3.0
(Councils)	(7)	(17)	(17)	(11)	(10)

rates. For this reason there is no easy way to tell from the data of Table 5–5 whether policy development indicates a victory for the high tax faction in a city, the more advanced age of a city, or forceful policy leadership by past city councils.

Improvements that city councils perceive their citizens to want provide a more typical test of the representative character of city policy decisions.[4] In comparison with Table 5–3, Table 5–6 shows amenities to be much more important as improvements desired by citizens than as problems perceived by city councils. As improvements, however, amenities are not related to the level of city policy development. Rather, there is a "permissive consensus" in favor of amenities spending: councils feel that their citizens

---

[4]Councilmen were asked the question "Now, looking toward the future, what one community-wide improvement, in your opinion, does this city 'need most' to be attractive to its citizens?" Coding rules for individual councils are described in Appendix B, p. 171.

would be happy to see more city amenities, whatever the present level of such programs. This being so, amenities expenditures can become a low priority item in the city budget. Because amenities do not arouse much political controversy, they need be provided only to the extent possible within the tax and spending limits that city residents impose on their government. City councils may exercise policy leadership in this area, but they are not required to take any particular action at any specific time.

As desired improvements, planning and zoning are conspicuously absent. Citizens are apparently more concerned (as councilmen see it) about streets, services, or urban renewal—the concrete results of city planning—than they are about planning in the abstract. As was true of city problems, renewal and redevelopment improvements of this kind are more often mentioned in cities at higher levels of policy development than in cities at lower levels. These facts indicate that city councils can use planning

Table 5–6
Improvement Suggestions and City Policy Development

Most frequently mentioned improvement councils perceive citizens to want	*Position in development typology*				
	Retarded	Emergent	Transi- tional	Maturing	Advanced
Urban renewal, industrial or commercial development	0%	14%	10%	14%	29%
Better services and streets	0	5	5	14	0
Better zoning	10	0	0	0	0
Better amenities	50	49	71	58	65
Mixed, none	40	32	14	14	6
	100%	100%	100%	100%	100%
(Councils)	(10)	(22)	(21)	(14)	(17)

and zoning as tools for meeting the expressed desires of city residents. Conflicts over planning are not conflicts over the idea of planning *per se,* but over particular directions of planning and growth.

Finally, it is interesting to note that the more advanced a city's policy, the greater its councilmen's agreement about the improvement their citizens want most. This relationship is shown by the declining percentage of cities coded "mixed or none" as city policy becomes more developed. The most likely explanation for this finding is that the idea of "city improvement" is less relevant for cities at low levels of policy development than for cities following more highly developed policies. Policy development is related to a commitment to improvement and change shared by citizens as well as city leaders, and a greater commitment increases the likelihood of agreement among councilmen regarding the specific improvements desired.

Council Leadership in Policy-Making

The style of city politics should change as the city changes, and these differences should be related to city policy development. Table 5–7 shows several measures of political style derived from interviews with councilmen in the San Francisco Bay region. First, split voting lineups become more common as policy becomes more developed, probably because city councilmen represent the increasing diversity of city residents and interests within the city.[5] Diversity of any kind appears on the council

---

[5] Voting lineups were coded from this question in the interview schedule: "When the Council is in disagreement on an issue, would you say there is more or less the same lineup of votes here in (city)? I mean, do some members seem to vote together on controversial issues? IF YES: With whom do *you* usually vote on controversial matters? Now, what about the others? Are they united or split? IF SPLIT: Who would you say votes most often together when the others are split?" The question allowed identification of three types of decisional structure—unipolar, bipolar, and nonpolar. As these adjectives suggest, a unipolar decisional structure is one in which all members always vote together, although there may be an occasional deviant. Bipolar structures are divided by a permanent split into two factions, although there may be

itself, since the sharpest break in the pattern occurs at a low level of policy development—between the Retarded and Emergent levels. These data clearly disprove any notion that a unified council is necessary for policy development. Split voting lineups are a direct result of city diversity, but they do *not* in turn seem to hamper the council's ability to pass policies to cope with the problems of a complex city.

We would also expect the city manager to become increasingly important in setting policy as cities become more complex, since government itself would become so complex in these municipalities that the council could make only the most cursory overview of its activities. This is true, according to Table 5–7, although a majority of councils at all levels of policy development insist that they make most policy decisions.[6] Dependence on the manager begins earlier than might be expected—between the Emergent and Transitional levels. This relationship provides evidence that some policy leadership in cities with advanced policies may be undertaken by the city manager rather than the city council.

Whether or not councilmen are always directly responsible for determining city policy, we would expect that their attitudes toward city change would be related to the policies their city is following. Two measures introduced in chapter 4, "favorability to change" and "future role of city government," are strongly related to city policy development, as shown in Table 5–7. In general, the more developed city policy is, the more favorable councils are to city change and an active role for city government. Both measures attain their highest value in Maturing cities and

---

"swing voters" who from time to time shift from one faction to the other. Nonpolar structures are those not exhibiting a recurrent voting pattern.

[6]Councilmen were asked to check one of five items, ranging from "manager initiates all policy proposals" to "council initiates all policy proposals." Only those items that did not mention the manager at all were presumed to indicate council initiation of policy, and a city was so coded if a majority of responding councilmen felt that the manager played no part in policy matters. Since each respondent interpreted for himself what was meant by "policy matters," the responses may overstate the actual amount of manager initiation of policy as defined in this study.

Table 5–7
Political Style and City Policy Development

Measure of political style	Position in development typology				
	Retarded	Emergent	Transi-tional	Maturing	Advanced
Council voting lineup is unipolar rather than split	90%	47%	33%	28%	19%
(Councils)	(10)	(21)	(21)	(14)	(16)
Council rather than manager makes policy proposals	75%	67%	58%	50%	60%
(Cities)	(8)	(21)	(19)	(12)	(15)
Median value, city change score	0.6	0.8	1.0	1.2	1.0
(Councils)	(10)	(22)	(19)	(14)	(17)
Median value, future role score	0.7	1.3	1.5	1.5	1.4
(Councils)	(10)	(22)	(19)	(13)	(15)
Orientation to action:					
Fatalistic	25%	33%	12%	8%	0
Pragmatic	75	27	76	59	50
Political	0	40	12	33	50
	100%	100%	100%	100%	100%
(Councils)	(8)	(15)	(17)	(12)	(14)
Budgetary style:					
Negative	43%	42%	56%	37%	46%
Rational	57	42	39	36	20
Formal	0	11	5	9	7
Programmatic	0	5	0	18	27
	100%	100%	100%	100%	100%
(Councils)	(7)	(19)	(18)	(11)	(15)

decline slightly in Advanced cities, indicating that the Advanced stage is in fact the terminal point for policy development.

Further, city councils acquire a favorable attitude toward a positive role for city government earlier than they become favorable to city change. As indicated in chapter 4, the explanation for this discrepancy is that many Emergent cities, where councils hold a positive future role but oppose change, are actively pursuing a restrictive zoning policy. The generally high future role scores in these cities indicate that many councils believe that they are taking an active part in their city's future regardless of how favorable to change they may be and how advanced a policy their city is following.

The leadership style of councils, as indicated by the manner in which they approach political action, also changes markedly as city policy develops.[7] Councils more often see themselves as leaders and educators of the public (the "political" orientation) in the final two levels of policy development than in the other three; also, councils in these two categories are much less likely to be fatalistic, i.e., to see city problems as being beyond their control.

Council orientations to action are particularly interesting in the light of council comments about policy initiation. In many Maturing and Advanced cities where the manager proposes policy measures but the council also adopts a "political" style, a form of reverse representation may be occurring: the manager initiates many new policies, and the council then exercises political leadership to persuade civic leaders and influential citizens that the new city policy is in the city's best interest. The more normal representational relationship probably operates in most cities, however: the council exercises policy leadership by interpreting and modifying citizen desires and then instructs the city manager to carry out new policy decisions.

Some behavioral confirmation for these general action orientations is provided by council budgetary styles. Table 5–7 shows

---

[7]Orientation to political action was a summary code made from the interview materials. It took into account questions relating to problems, improvements, future image, and budgetary style. Coding rules are described in Appendix B, p. 170.

that councils more often use the budget as a policy instrument (the programmatic style) in Maturing and Advanced cities than elsewhere. In all but the Retarded group some councils will defer to the manager on budgetary matters (the formal style), but the percentage is very small in all cases. Councils in cities with advanced policies are as likely to cut expenditures whenever possible (the negative style) as councils in other cities. Since the unit of analysis in this table is the council rather than the individual councilman, we can conclude that a programmatic budgetary style is conducive to policy development but not essential and that an orientation to budgeting stressing economy does not necessarily hinder policy development. These relationships are quite plausible, since the typology of policy development used in this study does not require high levels of total expenditure or consistent long-range spending plans, and they support the conclusions reached in chapter 4.

Summary: The Correlates of Policy Development

The gradual, and for the most part monotonic, changes exhibited by a wide range of variables in Tables 5–1 through 5–7 across the five policy types reinforce the assumption that these types do represent a sequence of policy development. The shape of the relationship differs somewhat from variable to variable, but many relationships rank the five policy types in the order shown. Because of this consistency, we can gain some idea of the relative importance of the several variables supposed to be causally related to city policy development.

Even though this sequence of policy development is not even remotely a continuous ratio scale of policy, some useful results can be obtained by treating it as if it were. The major requirements for making this assumption are that the dependent and independent variables not be strongly skewed from a normal distribution. The dependent variable meets this test reasonably well: if scores one through five are assigned to Retarded through Advanced policy outcomes, the mean value of the score for all cities is 3.1 and the standard deviation is 1.4.[8] Some of the independent variables are similarly distributed, while others are not. Variables whose standard deviation is quite high in relation to their mean value will be eliminated as nonsignificant by a t test.

A number of regression equations were calculated, using the independent variables in various combinations to find the set of variables that predicted policy development scores best. Table 5–8 summarizes the results of the fifteen most promising equations. The percentage of the total variance in the dependent policy variable "explained" by these equations varied from 43 to 71 percent.

A comment about interpreting Table 5–8 should be interposed here. An assumption underlying multiple regression analysis is that the independent variables are each more highly correlated with the dependent variable than with other independent variables. In fact, this is not always so. Those independent variables whose partial correlation coefficients and regression coefficients vary widely from equation to equation are being unduly affected by the other variables included in the equation. Judgments about the significance of these variables must therefore be tentative until their interrelationships with other independent variables are unraveled in chapter 6.

From Table 5–8 we can tentatively conclude that council perceptions are unimportant for policy development, except for

---

[8]There are at least three plausible ways to assign scores to the ten policy profiles:

	A	B	C
A–low, P–low	1	1	1
A–falling, P–low	2	2	2
A–rising, P–low	2	3	3
A–low, P–rising	2	3	4
A–high, P–low	3	4	5
A–low, P–high	3	4	6
A–high, P–falling	4	5	7
A–high, P–rising	4	6	8
A–rising, P–high	4	6	9
A–high, P–high	5	7	10

The product moment correlations among these three are A to B, .989; A to C, .983; B to C, .992.

Table 5-8

Statistically Significant Predictors of City Policy Development Scores: Results Obtained in Fifteen Regression Equations

Independent variable	Partial correlation with policy development score	Regression coefficient	Level of significance by t test*
Population density	−.07 to +.30	−.00002 to +.00016	I to .005
Population growth rate	+.20 to +.41	+.007 to +.012	I to .005
Change in population density	−.30 to −.39	−.204 to −.279	I to .05
Tax limit over $1 per $100	+.40 to +.69	+1.078 to +1.862	.025 to .0005
Assessed value per capita	−.01 to +.43	−.000006 to +.000321	I to .05
Perception of amenities problems	−.19 to −.62	−.027 to −.075	.05 to .005
Perception of tax base problems	−.16 to −.42	−.337 to −.807	I to .05
Future role score	+.09 to +.47	+.165 to +.844	I to .05

*"I" indicates insignificance at .05 level. All significance tests are one-tailed.

those relating to amenities problems and possibly tax base prob-lems. Both these perceptions display negative correlations with policy development scores, suggesting that cities with highly developed policies have encountered and dealt with amenities and tax base problems at some point in the past. The very strong relationship between policy development and a city tax limit over $1 per $100 supports the conclusion that cities with highly developed policies have somehow managed to escape the mone-tary restrictions that plague many cities at lower levels of policy development. But, since policy development does not necessarily imply higher expenditure burdens (as indicated in Table 5–1), the reason for the strong relationship between tax limits and policy development is not completely clear. In part, the high tax limit simply reflects the age of the city and the consequent likeli-hood that the city government has had experience in dealing with a number of problems in the past, but a higher tax limit may also be related to a desire on the part of the city council to take an active part in their city's future development. The plausibility of this argument is supported by the positive relationship in Table 5–8 between council future role scores and policy develop-ment, although this relationship is not as strong as that between tax limit and policy development.

Table 5–8 indicates that environmental pressures for policy development are related to policy development, although the conclusion for population density must be tentative because it is apparently strongly related to other independent variables. For both growth rate and density the relationship is positive, as would be expected for environmental variables regardless of the stage of the policy process that particular cities might happen to be in at the time of data collection. The actual significance of popu-lation growth is probably greater than that indicated by the results of these regressions, because population growth declines for cities with Advanced policies (see Table 5–2).

In addition to the level of population density, recent changes in density seem to be somewhat important for policy develop-ment. The relationship is negative, suggesting that city councils have already reacted to the pressures generated by increasing city density by boosting city expenditures. Yet it seems unlikely that city programs react so quickly to environmental changes. The negative sign of this relationship probably means instead that the pressures for policy development generated by increasing population density are being felt but that the programs to deal with these pressures have not yet been put into effect.

In addition to a high tax limit, cities with highly developed policies also seem to have a higher assessed value of real property per capita. We cannot conclude definitely that a high assessed valuation is conducive to policy development, however, because assessed valuation is also related to some other independent variable, as indicated by the fluctuating sign of the partial correlation between assessed valuation and policy development scores.

A number of variables not shown in Table 5–8 were also used in regression equations but were not significantly related to city policy development. The following variables were never statistically significant:

> urban realm position of city;
> council voting lineups;
> council perception of "paying for services" problems; and
> council perception of planning problems.

In addition, the following variables were not significant when density, growth rate, tax limit, and perception of amenities problems appeared in the same equation:

> council perception of desired amenities improvements;
> council perception of desired planning/zoning improvements;
> council favorability to city change;
> percentage of city revenue derived from the property tax; and
> level of per capita total expenditures.

Some of these variables would not be expected to correlate with policy development because no such correlation appeared in tables earlier in this chapter. Other variables were apparently

related to policy development, however, and their failure to predict policy development must be explained.

The urban realm relation is the easiest to explain because it
was not strongly correlated with policy development to begin with
(see Table 5–2). Apparently, the policy variation within realms
is greater than the variation between realms, so that the residual
effect of city realm position is not significant when the main effects
of density, tax limit, and other factors have been removed.

The insignificance of council voting lineups is also easy to explain. If voting lineups had any effect at all on policy development, they would probably hamper development by introducing
conflict and delay into the policy process. But Table 5–7 indicates
that the opposite relationship holds: cities following Advanced
policies also have more voting splits. One possible explanation
for this relationship is that voting splits do not appreciably delay
council decision-making; another is that the city manager makes
most of the policy decisions anyway. These splits are apparently
one aspect of the city policy process that reflects changes in city
environment but does not affect the ability of the city government
to deal with those changes.

Council perceptions of city problems and desired improvements present more difficulty. Having found no relationship between these measures and policy development for all eighty-four
cities, still we cannot be sure that there will be no relationship
for a subgroup of this population. In particular, council perceptions of problems and desired improvements should be most
important in cities undergoing policy change—totaling thirty-six
of the eighty-four cities for which complete information is available. The possibility that data for these cities are concealed by
that from cities where policy change is not occurring will be examined in chapter 6, but let us consider here some of the im-
plications of a city policy process in which city problems and
citizen desires are not important forces in policy development.

It is doubtful that the amenities desires of city residents could
ever be a very strong motivational force in the city policy process.
As Table 5–6 indicated, additional public amenities are desired
in many cities irrespective of their present level of availability.
Probably none of these cities really needs more amenities in the

sense that the city's social fabric will come apart or the incumbent council will be thrown out of office if more amenities are not provided. Thus any new amenities program or substantial increase in an old one will have to result from policy leadership by the council or city manager. Together or individually, they will be relatively free to make decisions because new programs, while not imperative, may be obviously desirable. Therefore, the insignificance of council perceptions of amenities improvement desires simply reflects the fact that amenities are not burning political issues in most cities.

Perceptions of planning problems or improvements are probably unimportant for several reasons. First, they are not often mentioned. Councilmen more frequently refer to specific kinds of city changes that planning might bring about than to planning or zoning in the abstract. Second, city councils are probably more closely constrained by environmental factors to adopt active planning and zoning policies than they would be for amenities expenditures. If this is true, environmental factors would be the direct cause of both planning problem perceptions and planning expenditures, and planning problem perceptions would add little to the explanation of planning expenditures offered by environmental factors like population growth.

Finally, policy leadership in the areas of planning and zoning —council policy decisions not made under overbearing pressure from environmental conditions or citizens—is probably more directly related to council leadership styles and council favorability toward an active role for city government than to problem perceptions. This conclusion is suggested in Table 5–8: future role scores are significant predictors of city policy development but favorability to city change is not. Favorability to city change implies that particular kinds of solutions must be found to city planning or zoning problems, but favorability toward an active role for city government does not (see Table 4–3). Consequently, the linkage of environmental factors to city policy will also involve planning problems perceptions and change favorability, but an active future role can and will be taken by city councils able to act freely and without too much constraint from environmental or other external factors.

We have yet to determine what conditions are most conducive to council policy leadership and under what circumstances the desires of city residents will be most directly implemented as city policy. The answers to these questions—to be sought in the next chapter—will also provide additional tests of many of the tentative conclusions advanced here.

Chapter 6

The Roots
of Policy Development

Categorizing Cities for Causal Analysis

The tentative nature of the conclusions in the last chapter was the direct result of examining the entire group of cities together. Only a few cities will be undergoing significant policy change during a given period. Further, amenities and planning policies probably develop at different times and at different rates in the same city. For these reasons we should examine amenities and planning expenditures separately, attempting to distinguish those cities undergoing policy change from the remainder whose policies are for the moment unchanging.

In general, this study has assumed that city councilmen respond to challenges from their city's environment and represent the wishes of their constituents. These linkages provide the causal element in a theory of city policy. Certainly the life styles sought by city residents do affect the kinds of amenities and planning policies followed by each city, as do the immediate desires and demands of citizens as perceived by city councils.

In addition to these causal factors, however, city councils may also exercise substantial discretion with regard to the timing, extent, and purpose of expenditures. City councils, in other words, are directly involved in setting the goals or purposes of city policy in addition to representing constituents. Dollar amounts do not by themselves reveal the purposes of particular planning or amenities policies, but the different purposes underlying public policy are reflected in weaker or stronger links between city policy measures and their correlates in different areas of the metropolitan region. In this chapter, inferences about purposive council behavior will be drawn from correlations of this kind.

The urban realm typology introduced in chapter 2 can serve as an appropriate device for roughly classifying cities according to their stage of development within the Bay region. At this point, however, it is desirable to merge some of the realm types; by doing so, we hope to make the model building procedure more reliable by increasing the number of cases used to calculate the necessary correlation coefficients. The following three groups of cities can be defined:

> CORE AREAS—traditional core and preautomotive industrial cities, prairie cities and noncentric industrial cities
> SUBURBS—railroad suburban cities and noncentric residential cities
> FRINGE AREAS—urbanizing cities and nonmetro cities

The justification for collapsing the realm typology in this way is based partly on theory and partly on the characteristics of these cities as summarized in Table 2–1. In the theory of city policy presented in chapter 1, core cities are the oldest, most densely and diversely settled in the region. Next in order come "prairie residential" cities, followed by railroad suburbs. Beyond these are the large postwar "noncentric" settlement areas and beyond them, the urbanizing areas. Farthest from the centers of the region are the nonmetro cities, those not in the path of metropolitan expansion and not strongly linked by employment opportunities to the regional centers.

The prairie residential cities can be classed with the core group because most have long been industrialized and as densely settled as many of the traditional core cities. Except for the somewhat higher social status of their population, prairie cities are therefore similar to older core cities, as Table 2–1 shows. Noncentric industrial cities are included in the core group because, theoretically, they seem to represent a phase of city ecological develop-

ment midway between suburbs and core areas. These are the
cities that have acquired, by choice or by accident, much of the
diversity of land use types and residential settlement character-
izing core cities. Consequently, they should have problems more
like those of core cities than those of suburbs, and they will be
treated as "emerging core cities" for the causal analysis in this
chapter. Obvious differences between traditional core cities and
noncentric industrial cities (dissimilar growth rates, for example)
must of course be kept in mind when interpreting the results.

Once the industrial cities have been separated from the noncentric group, the remaining noncentric residential cities look
very much like railroad suburbs; moreover, treating these two
groups together does little harm to the data.

Finally, the urbanizing and nonmetro cities are placed together
in the residual category. Theoretically, urbanizing cities represent
a phase of development between the nonmetro and suburban
stages. Actually, many councils in nonmetro cities worry about
impending development and metropolitan growth as much as
councils in urbanizing cities. Consequently, we may quite logically consider these two groups together in a study of the policy
process.

Some Causal Hypotheses

Having defined three broad groups of cities, we can now offer
some hypotheses to guide the examination of the data:

Fringe area cities are of two general types: older agricultural
cities or commercial centers for surrounding agricultural areas
and newer upper income residential "exurbs." Both types will
be threatened by metropolitan growth, but only the older cities
will actually be growing and changing significantly. For these
older cities, planning expenditures will be used to encourage
growth or at least to prepare for it and direct it, while in the
newer upper income cities planning expenditures will be used
to implement zoning policies designed to prevent growth. Residents in these new low density suburbs will not want publicly
provided amenities, but residents in the older and denser fringe

cities will probably want and need some form of public amenities. Thus, in fringe areas, planning allocations should be related to a positive future role for city government and to council perception of zoning problems. Amenities expenditures will be positively related to population density and also to council perception of development problems, since the older cities in the fringe group should be concerned with both development and public amenities.

Suburban cities are similar to some fringe cities in that they are largely residential and mostly upper income, but they differ in that they have already experienced some growth and are more concerned about channeling growth in desired directions than about preventing it completely. Thus, both a positive future role for city government and council perception of zoning problems will be related to planning expenditures in suburban cities but with the importance of zoning problem perceptions much less than in fringe cities. In suburban cities the public provision of amenities should be largely a matter of discretion for the city residents. Most suburbs are of medium density and moderate-to-high income levels, and there is little necessity for publicly provided amenities if the residents choose not to have them. Population density should also be important, however, because many of the older railroad suburbs were settled more densely than the newer automotive suburbs, and the need for public parks and recreational facilities should consequently be greater in these older cities. Thus, population density and council perceptions of citizen desires for amenities will both be related to amenities expenditures in suburban cities.

Core cities are the most diverse in their characteristics—both individually and as a group. The diverse character of most of these cities means that their governments will have difficulty using planning expenditures to direct their city toward a single clear set of goals. The diversity of city residents and the variety of their preferred life styles will also complicate the identification of a dominant popular sentiment by councils in these cities. Consequently, city planning expenditures in core areas will be used primarily to react to city growth and to deal with the redevelopment and urban renewal problems common to many core cities. For this group, the strongest predictor of planning expenditures will be population growth, especially because the rapidly growing noncentric industrial cities are included with the core group. The greater need for costly urban renewal programs, the expense of replacing old facilities and streets, and the pressure on existing services presented by rapid population growth in some core cities all suggest that alternative ways of spending city funds will compete more sharply in core cities than in suburbs or fringe areas. Thus, there may be many reasons for the existence of amenities programs or their absence. Population density should be important because there is a considerable spread of population densities within the core group. The absence of other major city problems, such as an inadequate tax base, may give some cities the freedom necessary to allocate large sums to amenities programs. Since the core area also contains a few small upper income residential enclaves, the amenities desires of city residents may also be important in a manner similar to their effect in suburbs. Which of these causes of amenities spending actually predominates will depend on the mixture of cities included in the core group.

Construction and Analysis of the Causal Models

For each city group a matrix of simple correlation coefficients was calculated by a standard computer program to determine which variables were most promising in constructing causal models for amenities and planning. From these larger matrices, a smaller set of variables was taken that included those measures correlating most strongly with either amenities or planning expenditures, plus some theoretically important variables regardless of the size of their correlation with the output measures. The construction of the council-level measures is described in Appendix B, p. 169. The correlations are included in Appendix C, p. 173.

Some of the variables are skewed—their standard deviations being greater than their mean values. This skewing will tend to inflate the value of correlation coefficients somewhat, but in no case is the standard error of the mean so high that a variable is completely unusable. We can assume, then, that the correlation coefficients in Appendix C will be reasonably accurate indicators of the strength of the relationship between two variables. A *t* test will also help to eliminate those variables about which reliable conclusions cannot be drawn.

The model-building procedure, described in Appendix C, does not assume the importance of any particular set of variables or any specified causal linkages, nor does it preclude the possibility that the same model will apply to all three groups of cities. Its technique is completely empirical rather than an attempt to match previously constructed models to the data. This procedure was followed for two reasons. First, the number of possibilities that would have to be considered would be very large if specific causal models were postulated in advance. Second, the exploratory character of this analysis recommended that the data should not be forced into preconceived causal configurations.

The empirically derived causal models are shown in Figures 6–1, 6–2, and 6–3. The arrows in each diagram indicate the direction of causal linkage. The absence of an arrow between any two variables indicates that there is no direct causal connection between them, although they may be indirectly related through a third variable. The sign attached to each causal arrow indicates whether the underlying causal relation is positive or negative.

Planning

The specific hypotheses concerning planning advanced earlier in this chapter are largely borne out by the data. In fringe areas, both the perception of zoning problems and a favorable attitude toward the role of city government are positively related to planning expenditures, with zoning problems strongly predominating. Zoning problems, in turn, are directly related to the assessed value per capita. Assessed valuation, which was included as a measure of city resources, seems instead to be more closely related to the "exclusivity" of residential settlement in a city. Thus, the correlation between median house value and per capita assessed

Figure 6–1
Policy Models for Fringe Cities

AMENITIES EXPENDITURES

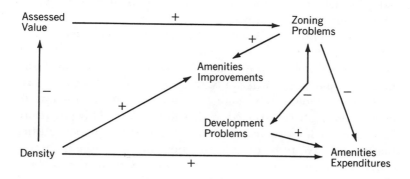

PLANNING EXPENDITURES

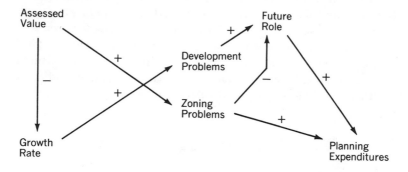

valuation is $+.75$ for fringe cities, and the correlation between median house value and perception of zoning problems is $+.84$. Any resource effects that might be measured by assessed valuation are therefore submersed by the much stronger relationship between assessed valuation and citizen life style preferences, which is opposite in sign to the relationship that would be expected if assessed valuation actually did measure city resources.

In suburbs future role scores and zoning problem perceptions are related to planning expenditures as hypothesized, but the

Figure 6–2
Policy Models for Suburbs

AMENITIES EXPENDITURES

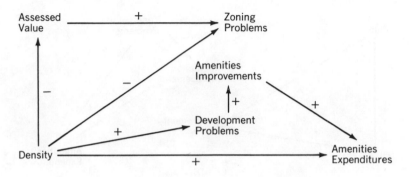

PLANNING EXPENDITURES

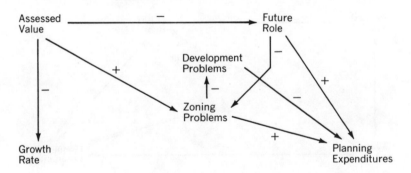

immediate causes of these council variables are different from those in fringe cities. Growth is independent of other model variables in fringe areas, but in suburbs it occurs primarily in cities with low assessed values and does not directly affect planning expenditures. This finding fits closely the expected relationships predicted earlier in this chapter. Since actual growth is no longer a major problem in suburban residential areas, planning policies need not react to city growth. Planning may be used instead to anticipate possible problems. Thus, planning is related

Figure 6–3
Policy Models for Core Cities

AMENITIES EXPENDITURES

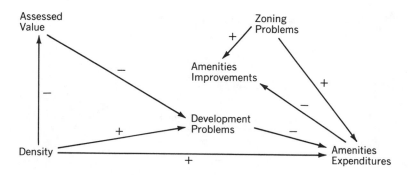

PLANNING EXPENDITURES

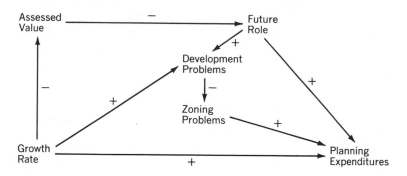

to perceived zoning problems and to the absence of council concern with city development. For another group of suburbs, those
with lower assessed valuations, planning policies implement a
council desire for an active city government, as shown by the
link from assessed value to future role scores and from future
role scores to planning expenditures.

In core and industrial areas, as hypothesized, planning expenditures are strongly related to city growth. The predominant
linkage is the direct one, indicating that planning is a reaction

to growth rather than an attempt to direct growth in order to deal with the problems of development or to follow particular concepts of the future role of city government. In fact, the effect of city growth on council attitudes toward the future role of city government is almost entirely mediated by a low assessed valuation: the correlation coefficient for this linkage is $+.12$, while that for the total relationship between growth rate and future role is $+.16$.

These findings can be more clearly understood by referring to the cities actually included in the core city group. The very rapidly growing cities in this group are the newer industrial cities located in the "noncentric" areas of the region. Their rate of population growth is so high that they are very much concerned about providing adequate water and sewage utilities to their new residents; thus, most of their planning budget is probably taken up with capital acquisition and bond scheduling, regardless of the kind of city the council desires. Growth does cause development problems in these cities, but development problems are only weakly related to city planning expenditures—suggesting again that the pressures of growth are a much more important cause of planning activity than council attempts to direct their city toward particular goals such as balanced land use. Only in suburbs, where the immediate pressures of growth are not so great, do perceived development problems become significant as causes of city policy.

Amenities

The three models derived empirically for amenities expenditures also closely follow the hypothesized relationships listed earlier in this chapter. In fringe areas, the more developed cities or those wishing to become more developed (as indicated by council perception of development problems) normally spend large sums on amenities. Here, the positive correlation between amenities expenditures and the perception of development problems probably does not in itself represent a causal linkage. Rather, it suggests that councils concerned about city development—renewing the downtown district, bolstering the tax base, or attracting industry—are also likely to be concerned about providing adequate amenities programs. Correlations offer some support for this hypothesis: for fringe cities, the future role of city government correlates with development problem perceptions $+.59$ when density is controlled, and future role scores correlate $+.31$ with amenities expenditures when density is controlled.

In suburbs, both density and perceived citizen desires for amenities improvements are related to amenities expenditures, as hypothesized. Causally, the impact of council perceptions of citizen desires for amenities improvements is completely independent of population density. We can probably safely infer, therefore, that these council perceptions actually do represent the desires of citizens in Bay region suburbs. Further, the positive sign of this relationship between spending and perceived desires indicates that in at least some suburbs the perceived desires of citizens accompany actual amenities programs such as parks and recreational areas or libraries. Our cross section of suburbs thus includes some cities where amenities programs are sufficient to satisfy low citizen desires for them and also some cities in the process of increasing their amenities expenditures in response to citizen desires. Both these relations are independent of, and in addition to, the effects of city density.

In core and industrial cities, the relationship between amenities improvement perceptions and amenities expenditures is the reverse of that in suburbs: the higher the level of amenities expenditures, the *less* frequently councilmen perceive amenities as an improvement desired by city residents. This finding suggests that these cities are, on the average, providing as much in the way of amenities programs of various kinds as the city councilmen think the citizens want. Thus, core cities are in the final stage of the policy formation cycle for amenities, having at some time in the past responded to citizen desires for amenities. Suburban cities in the Bay region, on the average, appear to be in the middle stages of this cycle, being in the process of responding to the perceived desires for amenities expressed by their citizens. For fringe cities, there is no direct relationship between amenities spending and perceived desires for amenities improvements, indicating that most of these cities are in the early stages of the policy cycle where spending is neither high nor strongly desired.

In addition to the relationship between amenities improvements and amenities expenditures, density in the core city group is also related to amenities expenditures. Thus, density is important in all three groups of cities, and in all cases it is positively related to amenities expenditures. In core cities, the *absence* of development problems is also related to the percentage of the total budget spent for parks, recreational programs, and libraries. Further, this relationship becomes much stronger when population density is controlled, changing from −.23 to −.46. Thus, as hypothesized, cities that have already dealt with problems relating to city development—urban renewal, a low tax base, or a lower-than-desired commercial and industrial development—are now free to spend money to provide amenities.

Core cities where zoning problems are perceived by city councils tend also to have high levels of amenities expenditures. Theoretically, there is no direct causal linkage between zoning and amenities, but the statistical relationship can be explained in terms of citizen life style preferences. Within a group of core and industrial cities, those cities concerned about zoning are probably old residential ones trying to retain their enclave status near the center of the metropolis. Since they were settled largely during the pre-automotive era, the density of settlement is fairly high. This can be seen by the absence of any relationship for the core group (r = +.07) between population density and council perception of zoning problems. Since population density is fairly high, the need for public amenities should be fairly high also. In addition to the level of amenities needs generated by population density, however, the residents of core cities of this kind apparently are favorably disposed to publicly provided amenities programs.

Causally, the relationship between zoning problems and amenities expenditures represents a real linkage between citizen desires and city amenities policy for core cities. Density exerts pressures for city amenities, and an absence of development problems allows city governments to take a more active part in providing amenities. But, in addition, citizen desires exert an independent influence on city amenities policy for at least some cities in the core and industrial category. The core cities to which this argument applies are similar to suburbs in social characteristics, reinforcing the argument that citizen desires are particularly important in "suburban" cities.

Summary: Predicting City Expenditures

These findings can be summarized in several ways. If we assume that each of the three city groups—core, suburbs, and fringe—is characterized by basically similar policy processes, then an attempt to explain the variance in policy outcomes in the three groups by the same set of variables will be appropriate. Table 6–1 summarizes the explanation of variance in amenities expenditures on the basis of the five independent variables used to formulate causal models for amenities. In these step-wise regressions the first five variables listed were forced into the regression first, the new variable added at each step being the one most strongly correlated with the residual variance. After all five of these variables had been used, additional variables were added—ending with a total of twelve for each regression.

In all three groups of cities, the first two or three model variables explain almost all the variance in amenities expenditures that the five model variables are able to explain operating together. For all groups, population density is overwhelmingly the best predictor, but the next most important variable is different from group to group. These step-wise regressions also offer additional confirmation for the policy models diagrammed for amenities expenditures in Figures 6–1, 6–2, and 6–3: those model variables most directly linked to amenities expenditures are also the variables that explain the most variance in amenities spending in the multiple correlations. For example, both Table 6–1 and Figure 6–1 show zoning problems, development problems, and density to be the most important predictors of amenities in fringe cities.

The model variables leave considerable unexplained variance in all three groups of cities. In all cases, the addition of new variables not in the model substantially reduces the unexplained variance, and many of the variables so added appear to be more powerful predictors of amenities expenditures than the model variables. For example, in suburban cities the percentage of total revenue derived from the property tax is a better predictor of amenities expenditures than the three least important model variables. The property tax rate is also significantly related to amenities expenditures in all three groups of cities.

Very similar observations can be made for planning expenditures from the data summarized in Table 6–2. Here, again, only a few of the model variables are strong predictors of planning expenditures in any one city group, but the important variables for each group are somewhat different. Council attitudes toward the future role of city government are important in all three groups, but they are the best predictor only in suburbs. For each group of cities, the model variables explaining the most variance are also the ones most closely linked to planning expenditures in the policy models in Figures 6–1, 6–2, and 6–3.

Here, also, additional variables "explain" much of the variance left after the five model variables have been introduced. For example, the level of total expenditures per capita is important in core and fringe cities, but not in suburbs. More detailed investigation of the suburban group would certainly be warranted, because the predictions for suburban amenities and planning expenditures are less accurate than those for core or fringe cities. The difficulty with suburb predictions is apparently *not* an inadequate model, however, because the addition of seven more variables does not bring the multiple correlation coefficient in suburbs up to the level of correlation achieved for core and fringe cities.[1]

The model relationships in this chapter can be summarized in another way. We can test the hypothesis that the actual "laws"

---

[1] The suburban group is certainly the most diverse and complex of the three city groups. There are noticeable interaction effects among the additional variables added to the suburban regressions. Thus, there are substantial causal linkages among these additional variables that could profitably be examined in more detail than is possible here. Apparently, however, more detailed analysis of the same variables would not lead to better prediction: variables not used in this study must be operating to contribute to the policies that suburbs follow.

Table 6–1
Multiple Correlations for Amenities Expenditures

Core Cities

Variable added		Multiple R^2 added	Significance level by *t* test*
(1) Density		.724	>.001
(2) Assessed value		.051	>.001
(3) Zoning problems		.026	.01
(4) Development problems		.002	I
(5) Amenities improvements		.001	I
	subtotal	(.804)	
(6) Per capita expenditures		.084	>.001
(7) Planning expenditures		.011	I
(8) Property tax rate		.015	.01
(9) Property tax revenue		.010	I
(10) Planning problems		.005	I
(11) City size		.005	I
(12) Growth rate		.002	I
		(.936)	

Suburbs

Variable added		Multiple R^2 added	Significance level by *t* test*
(1) Density		.584	>.001
(2) Amenities improvements		.069	>.001
(3) Zoning problems		.007	I
(4) Development problems		.005	I
(5) Assessed value		.000	I
	subtotal	(.665)	
(6) Property tax revenue		.042	.002
(7) Amenities problems		.009	I
(8) Property tax rate		.014	I
(9) Planning problems		.022	I
(10) Growth rate		.016	I
(11) City size		.020	I
(12) Favorability to change		.054	>.001
		(.842)	

Table 6–1 (continued)
Multiple Correlations for Amenities Expenditures

Fringe Cities

(1)	Density	.718	>.001
(2)	Development problems	.061	>.001
(3)	Zoning problems	.005	I
(4)	Assessed value	.006	I
(5)	Amenities improvements	.000	I
	subtotal	(.790)	
(6)	Growth rate	.041	.002
(7)	Planning problems	.028	.01
(8)	City size	.033	>.001
(9)	Property tax rate	.018	.02
(10)	Planning expenditures	.014	.05
(11)	Per capita expenditures	.004	I
(12)	Intergovernmental revenue	.002	I
		(.930)	

*"I" indicates insignificance at .05 level. Tests on the first five variables are one-tailed; tests on the remaining variables are two-tailed.

underlying city amenities and planning policies are the same for all groups of cities, as indicated by the regression coefficients.[2] These coefficients describe how much change in the dependent policy variable would be produced if a unit change were to occur in an independent variable. Such a law says nothing about what changes actually do occur in any variable for any group of cases, since this is determined solely by the cases examined. Thus, the relationship between city growth rate and planning expenditures, as measured by the regression coefficient, might be the same for all groups of cities, but the correlation coefficient could take on almost any value according to the amount of actual variation in growth rate or planning expenditures in a particular set of cases. For example, if Bay region suburbs have very similar rates of population growth, we would not expect the small differences

[2]The relative advantages of correlation and regression analysis are discussed in Hubert M. Blalock, "Causal Inferences, Closed Populations, and Measures of Association," *American Political Science Review* 61 (March 1967): 130–36.

Table 6–2
Multiple Correlations for Planning Expenditures

Variable added	Multiple R^2 added	Significance level by t test*
Core Cities		
(1) Growth rate	.727	>.001
(2) Future role of government	.123	>.001
(3) Zoning problems	.011	.05
(4) Development problems	.006	I
(5) Assessed value	.000	I
subtotal	(.867)	
(6) Per capita expenditures	.029	>.001
(7) Property tax revenue	.020	>.001
(8) Amenities improvements	.007	I
(9) Favorability to change	.007	I
(10) Planning improvements	.008	I
(11) Amenities problems	.006	I
(12) Planning problems	.007	I
	(.951)	
Suburbs		
(1) Future role of government	.460	>.001
(2) Zoning problems	.041	.02
(3) Development problems	.032	.05
(4) Assessed value	.001	I
(5) Growth rate	.000	I
subtotal	(.534)	
(6) Intergovernmental revenue	.157	>.001
(7) Density	.027	.05
(8) Per capita expenditures	.014	I
(9) City size	.008	I
(10) Favorability to change	.039	.01
(11) Amenities problems	.011	I
(12) Planning problems	.008	I
	(.798)	

Table 6–2 (continued)
Multiple Correlations for Planning Expenditures

Fringe Cities

(1) Zoning problems		.676	>.001
(2) Future role of government		.031	.05
(3) Assessed value		.000	I
(4) Growth rate		.000	I
(5) Development problems		.001	I
	subtotal	(.708)	
(6) City size		.120	>.001
(7) Per capita expenditures		.030	.01
(8) Planning improvements		.028	.01
(9) Intergovernmental revenue		.024	.01
(10) Planning problems		.004	I
(11) Favorability to change		.002	I
(12) Property tax revenue		.002	I
		(.918)	

*"I" indicates insignificance at .05 level. Tests on the first five variables are one-tailed; tests on the remaining variables are two-tailed.

in growth rate to predict much of the variance in planning allocations even if the underlying relationship is strong.

Table 6–3 shows the unstandardized regression coefficients for planning and amenities in the three city groups. The figures reported are calculated for zero intercept on the dependent variable, after all twelve variables shown in Tables 6–1 and 6–2 have been added to the regression model.

This table clearly shows that most of the independent variables are not consistently related to the policy measures they can be used to predict. Many of the regression coefficients are markedly different in the three city groups, not only in magnitude but also in direction. The property tax rate, for example, is positively related to amenities expenditures in fringe cities, more strongly positively related in suburbs, and negatively related in core and industrial cities.

Some relationships do seem to be almost invariant, however. City population density is consistently related positively to amenities spending. Here we have the explanation for the success with

Table 6–3

Regression Coefficients for Amenities and Planning

Amenities expenditures

Independent variable	Core cities	Suburbs	Fringe cities
Density	.00207*	.00223*	.00183*
Assessed value	−.00024*	.00131	−.00004
Amenities improvements	−.02108	.12216*	−.07654
Zoning problems	−.14713*	.08485	.15293
Development problems	−.07365	−.52874	.04068*
Growth rate	−.02459	−.08476	.08640*
City size	.00001	.00035	.00041*
Property tax rate	−10.36369*	17.57005	3.12280*

Planning expenditures

Independent variable	Core cities	Suburbs	Fringe cities
Growth rate	.05294*	−.02037	−.07291
Assessed value	.00017	.00048	.00001
Future role of government	2.24178*	3.44369*	3.33482*
Zoning problems	.23494*	−.00111*	.36476*
Development problems	−.07038	−.08587	−.05115
Per capita expenditures	−.00036*	−.00072	−.00028*

*Indicates significance at .05 level. Tests for first five variables in each group are one-tailed; remaining tests are two-tailed.

which amenities expenditures can be predicted from city density: the underlying relationship is similar in all groups of cities, and the variation in city density is fairly high in all three city groups. The future role of city government, council perception of development problems, and the level of per capita total expenditures are all consistently related to planning expenditures. A positive attitude toward the future role for city government, the absence of development problems, and a low level of total expenditures are all related to high planning allocations in all three groups of cities.

No pattern is apparent in the relationships that occur throughout the metropolitan region. City density is an aggregate characteristic of a city, representing a need (perhaps latent) for public amenities provision. City density is a permanent feature of city life that will not disappear or change even if the city council chooses to ignore it. On the other hand, council attitudes toward the future role of city government are susceptible to change independently of the city environment. A new election may bring into office councilmen with totally new outlooks without any corresponding change in city characteristics. The perception of development problems such as urban renewal or attraction of business and industry can also change with a change of councilmen, but it is somewhat more closely tied to actual city conditions than are council preferences regarding the future role of their government. The level of per capita total expenditures can also be determined to some extent by city councils, but they will be constricted by past commitments and certain minimum needs such as police and fire protection.

In short, the variables displaying consistent regression relationships with city policy are not of any one kind. They do tend, however, to be the most important predictive variables: density is the single most important variable in predicting amenities expenditures; future role is the single most important predictor of planning; and development problems and per capita expenditures are both useful in predicting amenities and planning allocations.

Independent variables that display a pattern of consistent change across the three groups of cities are also interesting theoretically. For example, in predicting amenities expenditures, the significance of zoning problems changes from positive to negative as one moves from fringe areas through suburbs to core areas. The importance of city size declines regularly to zero and the relationship between growth rate and city planning expenditures changes from negative to positive as one moves inward from fringe areas.

Although these relationships are generally not significant statistically, the fact that they are regular provides some support for the theoretical assumption that the three groups of cities represent different stages of metropolitan growth. The implication is not that any given city will eventually move through all stages found in the region but that movement between adjacent stages does involve ultimately irreversible ecological development. The fact that certain aspects of the policy process reflect this hypothesized sequence of metropolitan expansion strengthens the argument that the forces of metropolitan growth are important to city policy-making. Other factors may also be involved in the policy process, but they operate within the larger context of the whole metropolitan region.

Chapter 7

Conclusions:
Leadership and City Policy,
a Leap into the Future

Leadership Opportunities

Policy leadership has been an explicit organizing concept in this study. The underlying question of practical interest has been: how much control do political leaders have over their city's future? In answering this question, we have first explored the limits within which city councils work and then attempted to weigh the significance of the freedom of political action within these limits. Policy leadership can occur only when

1. an opportunity or a problematic situation exists;
2. political leaders perceive this opportunity or problem; and
3. political leaders are legally and politically free to choose among alternative courses of action in light of this opportunity or problem.

When these conditions are met, we can ask whether or not the formal political leadership of a city actually does take advantage of leadership opportunities. If it does not, we would want to know what overriding factors account for the decisions or nondecisions made. We would want to know, for example, whether city councils fail to perceive the problems their cities face or whether they are constrained by citizen demands or tax laws from taking action.

153

This study has focused on leadership in only one area of city government, namely, city policy designed to preserve, protect, or encourage a particular city life style in the face of the pressures of metropolitan expansion. The ultimate measure of policy leadership has been the presence or absence of amenities and planning programs, theoretically related to preferred city life styles. In this context, we can ask:

1. Which cities experience the pressures of metropolitan expansion or are confronted with the possibility of growth?
2. Do the councilmen in these cities perceive these problems or opportunities, and do they view them in policy terms?
3. Are these councilmen free to devise city policies to cope with these opportunities, or are they prevented from doing so by citizen demands, legal restrictions, or previous city development?

Chapter 2 dealt with the first two questions. Metropolitan expansion exerts several kinds of pressure on individual cities in the metropolitan region. Rapid population and land area growth, high density settlement, and urban decay are the concrete results of these pressures. Councilmen perceive these problems in their cities, but they also perceive a variety of other problems not directly related to the pressures of metropolitan expansion on the individual city. For example, many councilmen are concerned about smog control and rapid transit. These are not, strictly speaking, problems confined within the individual city's boundaries, and they are not susceptible to purely local solutions. Consequently, life style problems, opportunities to direct city growth, threats to open spaces, and urban redevelopment must compete in the councilmen's minds with numerous other problems, many of them area-wide in scope.

Nevertheless, the pressures of high growth and high population density are concentrated in some parts of the metropolitan region, and city councils in these areas are more concerned about these problems than councils in other parts of the region. High population densities are concentrated in the older cities near the center of the region and in a few older outlying cities. Rapid population growth is concentrated in a few areas on the outer edges of the metropolitan region and in the balanced and industrial suburbs settled since 1945. Core area councils mention urban redevelopment much more frequently than do councils in other parts of the region, and councils in rapidly growing cities mention growth and planning more frequently than other councils. We can conclude, first, that the pressures of metropolitan expansion do affect different cities in different ways, and, second, that these pressures are to some extent perceived by city councils.

In addition to the actual pressures of metropolitan growth, some city councils perceive the desirable or undesirable aspects of possible future growth. Councils in some older commercial cities on the fringes of the metropolitan region wish to attract more business, more industry, and more population to bolster their sagging economies. Councils in exclusive residential cities on the fringes of the region want to prevent growth in their cities, and they are worried because metropolitan expansion makes their cities prime targets for land developers. In both these groups of cities, there are strong links between environmental characteristics and policy-makers. Councils in these cities are agreed that the opportunities or threats from metropolitan expansion should be met by appropriate city policies.

Councilmen in core and suburban cities, on the other hand, do not always think in policy terms. To them, planning, parks, redevelopment, and zoning ordinances are "programs" rather than "policies." In other words, councilmen are much more likely to think in policy terms if a sudden need for markedly different city policies has arisen than if they have long been following similar policies. New challenges create opportunities for political leadership that may or may not be taken by city leaders.

Leadership situations may also arise even in old, slowly growing cities. The prime example here is urban renewal or renewal of the downtown business district. The need for redevelopment has been growing for many years, but a sudden recognition that something should be done about it constitutes an opportunity for policy leadership and policy change. An influx of new residents to an older suburb may also create a need for policy leadership. New residents may want more or different services,

and they may want the city to develop in a new direction. Councilmen must either change city policy or reaffirm old policy when
faced with a new political force in the community. In either case,
they must be conscious of what the present policy is and what
alternative policies are available.

Chapter 5 dealt in part with policy-related council attitudes.
Policy leadership, as indicated by highly developed city policies,
is related to council attitudes favorable to city change and a
positive future role for city government. Councils in cities with
advanced policies also tend to approach budgetary decisions from
a long-range, goal oriented viewpoint. There is some evidence,
however, that councils taking this "programmatic" approach to
budgetary decisions also articulate very general images of their
city's future—images that make little reference to patterns of land
use or life styles. The "policy" approach these councils take to
the budget also appears in many cases to be more general than
land use policies or development policies. Thus, even for the
few councils taking a programmatic view of budgetary decisions,
the budget is not in itself a useful instrument for policy leadership. When policy change is required, these city councils adopt
extraordinary procedures that enable them to make budgetary
decisions markedly different from those they would normally
make.

Limitations on Leadership

In general, the city policy process does not suffer from any
failure on the part of decision-makers to recognize the important
problems of their city. Thus, the first and second conditions for
policy leadership are met in Bay region cities. City policy-makers
may be unable to take appropriate action, however, because their
freedom to act may be limited in some way. Chapter 3 examined
the monetary limitations on city policy. These limitations come
from two sources: the actual inadequacy of the city tax base and
citizen demands for low taxes.

Council perceptions of citizen low tax demands are distributed
widely throughout the Bay region, although they are somewhat

less common in core cities. Councils are responsive to these demands, especially in cities with a narrow tax base. At the same time, however, responsiveness to these pressures does not preclude substantial amenities and planning expenditures. The funding of amenities and other "optional" programs simply makes cutting the budget easier for city councils whenever this becomes necessary. All councils want to cut city expenditures if they can, and a tendency toward budget cutting in response to citizen demands cannot be used to explain differential policy behavior among the cities in this study. The difficult decisions requiring policy leadership are made outside the framework of "normal" budgeting. Table 5–4 (p. 115) offers additional support for this assertion: although the property tax is less often viewed as an important budgetary consideration in Maturing and Advanced cities than elsewhere, it is still important in a majority of councils at each level of policy development.

Table 5–4 also shows that objective measures of city resources such as the market value of taxable property per capita and the extent of dependence on the property tax are not correlated with actual city policy. Thus, if we assume that costly and diversified city policies are evidence of council policy leadership, we can conclude that city tax resources do not constitute important limits on city leaders.

One further aspect of city resources should be investigated, namely, the legal constraints under which cities operate. Resources may be available to a city, but it may not be able to use them because of various legal constraints. Specifically, county assessment of property and a tax limit of $1 per $100 assessed valuation might be serious hindrances to a city council attempting to institute a costly policy change. Table 5–4 shows that county assessment cannot be a very serious limitation for city policy-makers, because all but a handful of cities use county assessment figures. The $1 tax limit, however, appears to be closely associated with low levels of amenities and planning expenditures.

In California, all tax rate limits may be raised; state law requires only that cities incorporated under certain legal forms secure their residents' approval before raising the tax rate beyond the set limit. City residents can limit the ability of their city councils to exercise policy leadership simply by voting against new tax levies. In the Bay region, newspaper reports reveal the great frequency with which city residents turn down tax increases and tax overrides. Cities with high levels of amenities and planning expenditures have somehow managed to obtain a higher tax rate limit, either through original charter provisions or through the exercise of council leadership. Quite possibly, more cities would be following "advanced" policies if their citizens were not as opposed to high taxes as they seem to be or if they did not have a powerful means of control such as the requirement that tax hikes be approved by referendum.

Finally, the internal politics of city governments may engender two limitations on council policy leadership. If the city manager actually makes policy decisions, or if the city council is split into voting blocs and cannot agree on policy choices, the opportunities for council leadership may be seriously curtailed. Table 5–6 (p. 119) shows that these conditions do not apply to Bay region cities. Councils in cities following the most advanced policies *more* often exhibit voting splits than councils in cities with less advanced policies. A majority of councils at every level of policy development say that they retain exclusive control of policy proposals. Councils in Retarded and Emergent cities tend slightly to credit themselves with more policy control than do councils elsewhere, but the relationship is so weak that we can safely conclude that the policy differences among Bay region cities are predominantly the result of city council decisions.

Leadership and Expenditures

The multiple regression analysis in chapter 6 suggests that city councils are much more limited by metropolitan pressures and citizen desires than had appeared probable in previous chapters. Aggregate factors like city density, city growth rate, and citizen life style preferences (as reflected in assessed valuation per capita) are the independent variables that cause a large part of both expenditure and council attitude variation. Council attitudes and perceptions explain only a small fraction of the total variance by themselves.

Aggregate variables are understandably important, since they represent the opportunities and problematic situations that call forth policy leadership. If density of settlement were low everywhere in the Bay region, there would be little reason for concern about the effect of high density on city life. Councilmen would not be called upon to devise imaginative solutions to the problems of high density living because these problems would not exist. Similarly, if cities never grew at a rapid rate, there would be little need for city planning. The most casual form of control of city land use could be exercised, and only minimum anticipation of future utilities needs would be necessary. Problems would never become so important that the council would be forced to revise its policies.

Of far greater interest, however, is our finding that citizen desires strongly influence council attitudes and perceptions, because this kind of linkage brings together the councilman-as-leader with the councilman-as-representative. For example, chapter 6 shows that the councilman's attitude toward the future role of city government is directly related to assessed valuation for core and suburban cities but only indirectly related for fringe cities. Future role attitudes predict 12 percent of the variance in planning expenditures in core cities and 46 percent of the variance in suburbs, but only 3 percent in fringe cities. Zoning problem perceptions are not directly related to assessed valuation in core cities, but they *are* directly related in suburbs and fringe cities. Zoning problem perceptions predict 1 percent of planning expenditure variations in core cities, 4 percent in suburbs, and 68 percent in fringe cities. These results suggest that council policy leadership is most effective when implementing the preferences of city residents, at least in the area of planning and zoning expenditures.

Relationships of this kind cannot be found for amenities expenditures. For one thing, no general council attitude such as the preferred future role of city government or favorability toward city change correlates very highly with amenities expenditures. The public provision of amenities is an element of the public life style of cities, but this aspect of public life style does not seem to be related to a more general set of goals that might serve as the basis for council policy decisions. We can argue, then, that councilmen will be most successful in exercising policy leadership when they formulate a set of general goals or attitudes that represent the interests of city residents. The interview data did not yield any variable of this kind for amenities expenditures.

Looking more closely at the regression models for planning expenditure in chapter 6, we can see that there are several representational relationships operating. Council perceptions of zoning problems are positively related to assessed valuation and planning expenditures; council attitudes toward the future role of city government are negatively related to assessed valuation and positively related to planning expenditures. The future role relationship is strongest in suburbs and reflects a desire for planned growth in lower income suburbs, while the zoning problems relationship is strongest in fringe area cities and reflects a desire on the part of high income residential cities to prevent growth through restrictive zoning. In both cases, the cities involved are relatively small and relatively homogeneous in character.

Councilmen are least successful in exercising independent policy leadership in the case of amenities policy in core cities. Density is a powerful predictor of amenities expenditures in core cities, followed by assessed valuation and zoning problems among the model variables. Most of these core cities are large and fairly heterogeneous, and a variety of policy preferences will probably be found among the citizens in each. The few high income cities in core areas to which the assessed valuation and zoning problems linkage does apply are more homogeneous and not as large as other core or industrial cities. In fact, they resemble suburbs more closely than they resemble other core cities. Consequently, the same kind of representative relationship may be operating here, but the few cities to which it does apply are obscured by the much larger group of cities in which it would be politically impossible.

City councils can exercise policy leadership only when they are politically free to do so. They must represent a fairly homogeneous constituency that has fairly clear policy preferences. They must devise a general set of city goals or operate with a general set of attitudes toward city change that represent their constituents' interests. They must recognize the opportunities and pressures that produce situations calling for a policy response. All these conditions are more likely to be met in smaller, newer suburbs or in outlying fringe cities of a metropolitan region than in industrial or core cities where a clear representative relationship and a clear set of city goals are more difficult to develop. When these conditions are not met, a city council is likely to be constrained by economic and political limitations and it will be forced to react to problems as they arise rather than to anticipate them.

These conclusions do not imply that city programs will necessarily be inadequate in the absence of active policy leadership by city councilmen. The core and industrial group follows the most ambitious amenities policies found among the region's cities. They are also more likely to undertake large-scale urban renewal projects and to coordinate their planning with regional planning efforts than are other cities in the region. But city "policy" is much less clear in these cities because the cities themselves are highly diversified and less susceptible to rapid change, and city government tends to react to problems rather than to anticipate them. Whether this approach is desirable for metropolitan cities in the long run is difficult to determine; at present, however, it seems to be the only course open to many of them.

Appendixes

Appendix A

Urban Realms
in the San Francisco
Bay Region

1. Traditional core areas and preautomotive industrial areas
2. Prairie residential areas—old streetcar suburbs
3. Railroad suburbs—older, high income commuter areas
4. Postwar automotive housing and industrial areas
5. Urbanizing areas and areas of imminent urbanization
6. Fringe areas—older cities at the periphery of the metropolitan complex and isolated from the metropolitan economy

Map and classification adapted, by permission, from James E. Vance, Jr., *Geography and Urban Evolution in the San Francisco Bay Area* (Berkeley: Institute of Governmental Studies, 1964). Realm boundaries have been drawn to correspond roughly to the state of regional development in 1965.

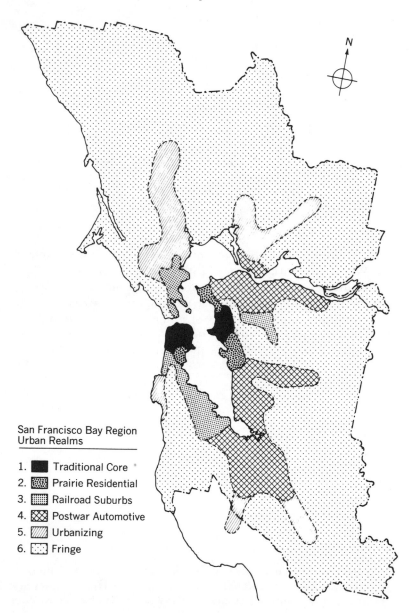

San Francisco Bay Region
Urban Realms

1. Traditional Core
2. Prairie Residential
3. Railroad Suburbs
4. Postwar Automotive
5. Urbanizing
6. Fringe

Appendix B

Data Sources
and Construction
of Council Measures

Aggregate Data Sources

City population, 1960:
U.S. Census of Population, 1960.

City population, 1965:
Estimates by California State Controller applicable to June 30, 1965, published in *Annual Report of Financial Transactions Concerning Cities of California* for fiscal year 1964–1965.

City land area, 1961 and 1965:
Estimates made in 1961 and 1965 by California State Division of Highways.

City population density, 1965:
Estimates made by California State Division of Highways.

City land undeveloped, 1965:
Estimates of all incorporated land not in urban uses, based on a land use survey by census tracts furnished by the Data Service of the Association of Bay Area Governments.

City land commercial or industrial, 1965:
Estimates of all urbanized incorporated land in commercial or industrial use, based on a land use survey by census tracts furnished by the Data Service of the Association of Bay Area Governments.

Per capita assessed property value, 1965:

Total assessed value of property subject to local property taxes, reported in *Annual Report of Financial Transactions Concerning Cities of California* for fiscal year 1964–1965.

Per capita market value of real property, 1965:

Per capita assessed property value for 1965 multiplied by the assessment ratio for each city ("Collier factor"), reported in *Annual Report of the California State Board of Equalization* for fiscal year 1964–1965.

Median value of owned homes, 1960:

U.S. Census of Housing, 1960 (average value of owned homes used for cities under 2500 population).

Employed residents in white collar occupations, 1960:

U.S. Census of Population, 1960.

Median family income, 1960:

U.S. Census of Population, 1960.

Expenditure and Revenue Data Sources

Per capita city government expenditures, 1965:

Total expenditures, reported in *Annual Report of Financial Transactions Concerning Cities of California* for fiscal 1965–1966, divided by city population in 1965.

Amenities expenditures for fiscal years:

Expenditures for parks and recreational facilities, libraries, and health services expressed as a percentage of total expenditures, based on *Annual Reports of Financial Transactions Concerning Cities of California*. Figures were also calculated using total expenditures less general government expenditures as the percentage base; for fiscal 1965–1966 the correlation between these two sets of figures was +.989.

Planning expenditures for fiscal years:

Planning commission expenditures expressed as a percentage of general government expenditures, based on *Annual Reports of Financial Transactions Concerning Cities of California*. Figures were also calculated using general government expenditures less debt service as the percentage base; for fiscal 1965–1966 the correlation between these two sets of figures was +.981.

Property tax rate, 1965:
Annual Report of Financial Transactions Concerning Cities of California for fiscal year 1964–1965.

Property tax revenue, 1965:
Annual Report of Financial Transactions Concerning Cities of California for fiscal year 1965–1966.

Intergovernmental revenue, 1965:
All grants and rebates from county, state, and federal sources, reported in *Annual Report of Financial Transactions Concerning Cities of California* for fiscal year 1965–1966.

Construction of Council Measures

Favorability to city change:
In a group of councilmen, that percentage whose future image involved a basic change in the nature of the city, planning for city change, or continuation of present change. Those who did not favor change held future images involving control of city change, slight changes to perfect their city, or no change at all.

City change score:
For each city, score two points for each respondent who wants to plan for change or wants a major change in the nature of the city, one point for each respondent who wants change to continue as at present or wants only minor changes in the city, and no points for each respondent who wants no change or wants to prevent change. The total score is then divided by the number of respondents in that city.

Future role score:
Councilmen chose one of the following statements:
"I would like to see the city cutting back on many of its more expensive programs."
"I would like to see the city paying off most of its debts

while maintaining its present level of services to citizens."

"I would like to see the city maintaining its present
level of activities."

"I would like to see the city providing more services to
its citizens than it does now."

"I would like to see the city government taking an active
part in promoting city growth."

Score no points for any of the first three responses, one point
for the fourth response, and two points for the last response.
The total score is then divided by the number of respondents
in the group.

Importance of the property tax in budgeting:

Respondents answered either "yes" or "no"; tied responses
on a council were coded "yes."

Most frequently mentioned improvement perceived to be desired
by citizens:

Each response is counted equally. A council is coded as
"mixed" if there is a tie between two or more response categories; otherwise, the most frequently mentioned category
is coded.

Orientation to action:

This is a summary coder judgment based on city problems,
future image, and budgetary behavior questions. A "political" orientation was one characterized by an emphasis on
leadership or compromise. A "pragmatic" or "instrumental"
orientation emphasized planning, the making of expenditure
decisions, or finding the appropriate means for a given goal.
A "fatalistic" orientation emphasized forces beyond the control of the council and included a general inability to act.
A council was coded as "none" if the responses were spread
among all three types of orientation; otherwise, the most
frequently occurring type was coded. For ties the priority
of coding was "political," then "fatalistic," then "pragmatic."

Budgetary style:

Individual councilmen were coded as "negative," "formal,"
"rational," or "programmatic." A council was coded as

"none" if at least two councilmen fell into each of three categories; otherwise, the most frequently occurring style was coded. For ties the priority of coding was "programmatic," then "formal," then "rational," then "negative."

Perception of amenities problems:
> For each council, the number of amenities problem responses expressed as a percentage of all problem responses.

Perception of planning problems:
> For each council, the number of planning problem responses expressed as a percentage of all problem responses.

Perception of zoning problems:
> For each council, the number of zoning problem responses expressed as a percentage of all problem responses.

Perception of tax base problems:
> For each council, the number of tax base problem responses expressed as a percentage of all problem responses.

Perception of development problems:
> For each council, the number of development problem responses (all responses relating to attraction of business and industry, urban renewal and urban redevelopment, or a low tax base) expressed as a percentage of all problem responses.

Perception of problems in paying for services:
> For each council, the number of "paying for services" problem responses expressed as a percentage of all problem responses.

Perception of amenities improvements desired by city residents:
> For each council, the number of amenities improvement responses expressed as a percentage of all improvement responses.

Perception of planning or zoning improvements desired by city residents:
> For each council, the number of planning or zoning improvement responses expressed as a percentage of all improvement responses.

Relative importance of conflicts among citizens:

Each councilman was asked to rank the relative importance of the following conflicts:

Business vs. labor

Republicans vs. Democrats

Old residents vs. new residents

White people vs. minorities

Supporters of new taxes vs. opponents

New subdivisions vs. old part of city

Liberals vs. conservatives

Supporters of city planning vs. opponents

For each council and for each conflict, code the rank assigned by a majority of respondents, recording the lower numbered rank in case of ties. If there is no majority agreement, code the average ranking, except that if all existing rankings for a conflict are four or lower, code a rank of nine. If a majority of respondents do not rank a given conflict, do not code a ranking for it.

Appendix C

Building Policy Process Models

Table C-1

Variables Used in Causal Model Construction

Core Cities

Variable Name	Mean value	Standard deviation	Standard error	Number of cases
Growth rate (%)	41.6	52.0	9.8	28
Population/sq. mile	3949.2	2956.5	588.7	28
Assessed value ($)	3339.0	4459.6	842.8	28
Perception of amenities improvements	46.1	28.6	5.6	26
Attitude toward future role of government	1.2	0.6	0.1	25
Perception of zoning problems	4.4	8.0	1.6	26
Perception of development problems	22.8	19.6	3.8	26
Amenities spending (%)	12.4	7.8	1.5	28
Planning spending (%)	4.4	4.1	0.8	28

Table C–1 (continued)

Suburbs

Variable Name	Mean value	Standard deviation	Standard error	Number of cases
Growth rate (%)	25.2	23.2	3.9	36
Population/sq. mile	3400.6	2147.4	357.9	36
Assessed value ($)	2645.3	1287.3	214.5	36
Perception of amenities improvements	49.5	27.6	4.7	35
Attitude toward future role of government	1.1	0.6	0.1	31
Perception of zoning problems	13.6	15.8	2.7	35
Perception of development problems	12.7	12.5	2.1	35
Amenities spending (%)	9.4	7.5	1.3	36
Planning spending (%)	6.3	7.3	1.2	36

Fringe Cities

Variable Name	Mean value	Standard deviation	Standard error	Number of cases
Growth rate (%)	20.4	24.7	5.0	24
Population/sq. mile	1940.3	1199.6	239.9	25
Assessed value ($)	2092.5	1089.4	217.9	25
Perception of amenities improvements	36.7	24.5	5.1	23
Attitude toward future role of government	1.2	0.6	0.1	23
Perception of zoning problems	6.8	11.5	2.4	23
Perception of development problems	10.2	12.4	2.6	22
Amenities spending (%)	8.0	6.7	1.3	25
Planning spending (%)	3.5	5.3	1.1	25

Table C–2
Simple Correlations Among Model Variables

Core Cities	(1)	(2)	(3)	(4)	(5)	(6)	(7)	(8)	(9)
(1) Growth rate	1.00	−.28	−.24	.04	.16	−.09	.26	−.29	.74
(2) Density		1.00	−.36	.07	.08	.07	.25	.55	−.17
(3) Assessed value			1.00	−.12	−.49	−.02	−.33	−.29	−.29
(4) Amenities improvements				1.00	−.09	.10	.26	−.16	−.08
(5) Future role					1.00	−.03	.20	.08	.47
(6) Zoning problems						1.00	−.19	.29	.12
(7) Development problems							1.00	−.23	.15
(8) Amenities spending								1.00	−.07
(9) Planning spending									1.00

Suburbs	(1)	(2)	(3)	(4)	(5)	(6)	(7)	(8)	(9)
(1) Growth rate	1.00	−.21	−.32	.24	.20	−.09	−.10	−.05	.08
(2) Density		1.00	−.23	.00	.26	−.37	.42	.28	−.32
(3) Assessed value			1.00	−.02	−.57	.53	−.28	−.09	−.15
(4) Amenities improvements				1.00	.09	−.01	.16	.19	.09
(5) Future role					1.00	−.53	.05	.04	.30
(6) Zoning problems						1.00	−.31	−.03	.05
(7) Development problems							1.00	.07	−.29
(8) Amenities spending								1.00	−.19
(9) Planning spending									1.00

Table C–2 (continued)
Simple Correlations Among Model Variables

Fringe Cities	(1)	(2)	(3)	(4)	(5)	(6)	(7)	(8)	(9)
(1) Growth rate	1.00	.10	−.31	.27	.30	−.10	.46	.44	−.03
(2) Density		1.00	−.50	.27	.13	−.31	.27	.57	−.14
(3) Assessed value			1.00	.08	−.54	.50	−.27	−.35	.37
(4) Amenities improvements				1.00	−.09	.19	.10	.14	−.00
(5) Future role					1.00	−.63	.60	.33	−.40
(6) Zoning problems						1.00	−.34	−.42	.75
(7) Development problems							1.00	.53	−.22
(8) Amenities spending								1.00	−.19
(9) Planning spending									1.00

The model-building procedure involved the following operations:

1. Find the highest simple correlation with the dependent policy variable in question—amenities, for example.
2. Assume that this variable is directly linked to amenities expenditures. Suppose, for example, this variable is density.
3. Partial out the effect of density: form the partial correlations between amenities and the other independent variables with density controlled.
4. Examine these partial correlations to determine whether density accounts for the relationship or not. For example, if the partial correlation of assessed value and amenities with density controlled is reduced to zero, density either causes assessed value or intervenes between assessed value and amenities. If the correlation is reduced, but not to zero, assessed value can be assumed to be directly related to amenities in addition to that portion of its relationship accounted for by density. If the correlation is increased, assessed value can be assumed to be an independent cause of amenities expenditures.

5. Using the relationships suggested in step four, construct a partial causal model and formulate testable predictions from it. For example, if both assessed value and amenities improvements are assumed to be caused by density, the partial correlation between assessed value and improvements would reduce to zero when density is controlled.

6. Check the predictions made in step five against calculations based on the data. Correct the provisional model, if necessary, to account for the actual partial correlations.

7. Continue to add new variables and revise the model as described above until all variables have been incorporated in the model and predictions from the model match the data closely.

Since the model is empirically derived from the data, there is no independent check on its suitability, but it is possible to demonstrate that the model for a given group of cities fits the data for those cities better than it fits the data for the other city groups. For example, using the reference numbers from Table C–2, we can make the following predictions for suburbs:

1. prediction: $r_{68.2} = 0$

actual values:	core cities	.30	errors:	.30
	suburbs	.08		.08
	fringe cities	−.31		.31

2. prediction: $r_{48.2} > r_{48}$

actual values:	core	−.23	−.16	errors:	yes
	suburbs	.20	.19		no
	fringe	−.02	.14		yes

3. prediction: $r_{38.2} = 0$

actual values:	core cities	−.12	errors:	.12
	suburbs	−.03		.03
	fringe cities	−.09		.09

For all three predictions, the data for suburban cities fit the expected findings better than the data for core and fringe cities. Similar demonstrations could be made for each empirically derived model.

Appendix D

Bibliographic Essay on Policy Studies, with Special Reference to City Policy

Since public policy can be regarded as an output of the political system, it is theoretically related to all other aspects of politics. Therefore, much political science research that does not take public policy as its explicit focus may nonetheless contain valuable insights regarding the formation of policy choices. In this brief essay references have been loosely organized according to the types of variables they emphasize, whether these are directly related to public policy or not.

Surveys of the urban studies literature include Jack P. Gibbs, ed., *Urban Research Methods* (Princeton: Van Nostrand, 1961); H. Wentworth Eldredge, ed., *Taming Megalopolis* (Garden City, N.Y.: Doubleday Anchor, 1967), 2 vols.; and Leo F. Schnore, ed., *Social Science and the City* (New York: Praeger, 1968). Charles M. Bonjean and David M. Olson review the community power literature in "Community Leadership," *Administrative Science Quarterly* 9 (December 1964). *City Politics and Public Policy* (New York: John Wiley & Sons, 1968), edited by James Q. Wilson, presents a collection of recent studies aimed specifically at city policy. Herbert Jacob and Michael Lipsky, "Outputs, Structure and Power," in Marian D. Irish, ed., *Political Science: Advance of the Discipline* (Englewood Cliffs, N.J.: Prentice-Hall, 1968), surveys a wide range of output studies at the city and state levels.

Many political studies concentrate on the process of decision. Case studies, in particular, focus on important policy changes or normatively significant decisions. *State and Local Government: A Case Book* (Birmingham: University of Alabama Press, 1963), edited by Edwin A. Bock, provides a good sample of well-written cases on city politics. Edward C. Banfield in his book *Political Influence* (New York: The Free Press of Glencoe, 1961); Warner E. Mills, Jr., and Harry R. Davis in *Small City Government* (New York: Random House, 1962); and Roscoe C. Martin *et al.* in *Decisions in Syracuse* (Bloomington: Indiana University Press, 1961) offer comparisons of several cases occurring in the same city. Wallace Sayre and Herbert Kaufman, *Governing New York City* (New York: Russell Sage Foundation, 1960) should also be consulted for its emphasis on the elements common to all big-city policy decisions. Robert L. Crain, Elihu Katz, and Donald B. Rosenthal, *The Politics of Community Conflict* (Indianapolis: Bobbs-Merrill, 1968) compares a number of community decisions relating to water fluoridation. *The Politics of School Desegregation* (Chicago: Aldine, 1968) by Robert L. Crain takes a similar approach.

An area in which comparison of process models has proved fruitful is the theory of allocation decisions and its political outgrowth, budgetary theory. David Braybrooke and Charles E. Lindblom, in *A Strategy of Decision* (New York: The Free Press of Glencoe, 1963), outline a technique for incremental, nonprogrammatic decisions. *Planning Programming Budgeting* (Chicago: Markham Publishing Company, 1967), edited by Fremont J. Lyden and Ernest G. Miller, explores the alternative, synoptic model of budgeting. John Patrick Crecine's *Governmental Problem Solving: A Computer Simulation of Municipal Budgeting* (Chicago: Rand McNally, 1969) refers specifically to city decisions. Another promising approach, yet to be applied to city politics, is contained in Otto A. Davis, M. A. H. Dempster, and Aaron Wildavsky, "A Theory of the Budgetary Process," *American Political Science Review* 60 (September 1966). Alan Altshuler describes city planning decisions in *The City Planning Process*

(Ithaca: Cornell University Press, 1965). Sidney M. Willhelm's *Urban Zoning and Land-Use Theory* (New York: The Free Press of Glencoe, 1962) should also be consulted for a political interpretation of planning decisions.

A second major class of policy-relevant studies focuses on decision-makers themselves. Individual legislative votes have been exhaustively analyzed by Duncan MacRae, Jr., *Dimensions of Congressional Voting* (Berkeley and Los Angeles: University of California Press, 1958) and David B. Truman, *The Congressional Party* (New York: John Wiley & Sons, 1959), among others. Warren E. Miller and Donald E. Stokes, "Constituency Influence in Congress," *American Political Science Review* 57 (March 1963) uses interview data imaginatively to develop causal models for legislative voting on various issues. Prediction of roll call voting has also been attempted by Cleo H. Cherryholmes and Michael J. Shapiro, *Representatives and Roll Calls* (Indianapolis: Bobbs-Merrill, 1969). Role orientations taken by legislators serve as explanatory variables in John C. Wahlke *et al., The Legislative System* (New York: John Wiley & Sons, 1962). A similar approach has been applied to local governmental bodies by James David Barber in *Power in Committees* (Chicago: Rand McNally, 1966).

Some studies of public policy concentrate on factors in the environment of the decision unit in question rather than on characteristics of decision-makers as major predictive variables. Regression studies of state, city, or school district expenditures provide the clearest examples of this kind of approach. Harvey E. Brazer, *City Expenditures in the U.S.* (New York: National Bureau of Economic Research, 1959) is a classic study. Otto Davis and George H. Haines, Jr., in "A Political Approach to a Theory of Public Expenditure: The Case of Municipalities," *National Tax Journal* 19 (September 1966) attempt to test political hypotheses through the use of aggregate data. Richard E. Dawson and James A. Robinson, "Inter-Party Competition, Economic Variables, and Welfare Policies in the American States," *Journal of Politics* 25 (May 1963); Thomas R. Dye, *Politics, Economics and the Public* (Chicago: Rand McNally, 1966); and H. Thomas James, James A. Kelly, and Walter I. Garms, *Determinants of Educational Expenditures in Large Cities of the United States*

(Stanford: Stanford University School of Education, 1966) all weigh the relative importance of political and environmental factors as causes of expenditures.

Environmental factor approaches to city policy also include the typologies of cities made by urban sociologists and urban geographers. William F. Ogburn, *Social Characteristics of Cities* (Chicago: International City Managers Association, 1937) and Howard J. Nelson, "Some Characteristics of the Population of Cities in Similar Service Classifications," *Economic Geography* 33 (April 1957) are early examples. *American Cities, Their Social Characteristics* (Chicago: Rand McNally, 1965) by Jeffrey K. Hadden and Edgar F. Borgatta uses factor analysis to summarize the relationships among a large number of city characteristics but does not specifically discuss public policy.

Studies such as Charles S. Liebman, "Functional Differentiation and Political Characteristics of Suburbs," *American Journal of Sociology* 66 (March 1961); John H. Kessel, "Governmental Structure and Political Environment," *American Political Science Review* 56 (September 1962); and Leo F. Schnore and Robert R. Alford, "Forms of Government and Socioeconomic Characteristics of 300 Suburbs," *Administrative Science Quarterly* 8 (June 1963) relate a city's social and economic activities to its governmental structure. James Q. Wilson and Edward C. Banfield, "Public Regardingness as a Value Premise in Voting Behavior," *American Political Science Review* 58 (December 1964) demonstrates the importance of differing value systems among city residents. Robert R. Alford and Harry M. Scoble in *Bureaucracy and Participation: Political Culture in Four Wisconsin Cities* (Chicago: Rand McNally, 1969) relate a city's economic base to the style of local political activity of its citizens.

The literature of political development provides a useful theoretical approach to city policy by emphasizing the effects of policy outputs on the political system as a whole. Representative works in this area include David Easton, *A Systems Analysis of Political Life* (New York: John Wiley & Sons, 1965); Lucian W. Pye, *Aspects of Political Development* (Boston: Little, Brown, 1966); and Robert T. Holt and John G. Turner, *The Political Basis of Economic Development* (Princeton: Van Nostrand, 1966).

Empirical studies using a similar approach include Henry J. Schmandt and G. Ross Stephens, "Measuring Municipal Output," *National Tax Journal* 13 (December 1960) and Donald J. McCrone and Charles F. Cnudde, "On Measuring Public Policy" in Robert E. Crew, Jr., ed., *State Politics* (Belmont, Calif.: Wadsworth Publishing Company, 1968).

Similar to developmental approaches and more directly relevant to city policy are a number of studies generally classified as "political economy." Charles M. Tiebout, "A Pure Theory of Local Expenditures," *Journal of Political Economy* 64 (October 1956) and Alan Williams, "Optimal Provision of Public Goods in a System of Local Government," *Journal of Political Economy* 74 (February 1966) discuss the theoretical basis for local governments. The Williams article also contains a valuable bibliography on economic approaches to city policy. Julius Margolis in "Municipal Fiscal Structure in a Metropolitan Region," *Journal of Political Economy* 65 (June 1957) uses demographic and expenditure data to identify the fiscal strategies used by cities in a single metropolitan region. Robert C. Wood, *1400 Governments* (Cambridge, Mass.: Harvard University Press, 1961) and Oliver P. Williams and Charles R. Adrian, *Four Cities: A Study in Comparative Policy Making* (Philadelphia: University of Pennsylvania Press, 1963) describe city policy outputs as strategies for preserving the differing values held by city residents. Oliver P. Williams et al., *Suburban Differences and Metropolitan Policies* (Philadelphia: University of Pennsylvania Press, 1965) relates city policies both to the values of city residents and to the specific economic functions performed by each city in the metropolis. Two collections of writings from the political economy viewpoint are Howard G. Schaller, ed., *Public Expenditure Decisions in the Urban Community* (Washington, D.C.: Resources for the Future, 1963) and Julius Margolis, ed., *The Public Economy of Urban Communities* (Washington, D.C.: Resources for the Future, 1965).

Appendix E

The Research Project and the Data

This Appendix provides a brief description of the context for the analyses and interpretations reported in this and the other monographs of *The Urban Governors* series. These analyses and interpretations are grounded in or inspired by data collected at a specific "point" in time—actually over a period of some eighteen months, from January 1966 to June 1967—in a particular region of the United States. The data are "representative," therefore, in only a very limited sense. Although none of the writers of the monographs would claim greater universality for his interpretations than the data warrant, the temptation on a reader's part to forget or ignore the limitations of a clearly bounded space-time manifold is always present. The reader is entitled, therefore, to information about the setting of each study, if only for comparison with settings which are more familiar to him and which serve as his own frames of reference.

Needless to say, we cannot describe here the San Francisco Bay metropolitan region, its cities and its people, in their full richness and diversity. Clearly, only certain aspects of the environment are relevant, and this relevance must be determined by the objectives of the particular research project in which we were engaged. Before presenting the relevant context, therefore, the research project itself will be described in brief outline.

The City Council Research Project

As mentioned already in the Preface, the Project was a research and training program with as many as twelve participants working together at one time. Because the Project was intended, from the beginning, to maximize the independent research creativity of each participant, the research design had to be sufficiently flexible to permit the collection of data which would satisfy each Project member's research concerns. The monographs in this series reflect the heterogeneity of the research interests which found their way into the Project. At the same time, each researcher was necessarily limited by the Project's overall objective, which was, throughout, to gather data which would shed light on the city council as a small political decision-making group.

Our interest in the city council as a decision-making group stemmed from prior research on governance through democratic legislative processes. Political scientists have been traditionally concerned with the variety of "influences," external to the legislative body as well as internal, that shape both the legislative process and the legislative product. It was an assumption of the research that these influences could be studied more intensively in the case of small bodies than in the case of larger ones, like state legislatures or Congress, that already have been widely investigated. In particular, it was assumed that a decision-making body is both the sum of its parts and greater than the sum of its parts. Therefore, both the council as a collective unit and the councilman as an individual unit could be selected for the purposes of analysis. In the major book of this series, by Heinz Eulau and Kenneth Prewitt, the council as such serves as the unit of analysis. In the accompanying monographs, individual councilmen primarily serve as the units.

Convenience apart, the choice of the universe to be studied was dictated by the research objective. On the one hand, we needed a sufficiently large number of decision-making groups to permit systematic, quantitative, and genuinely comparative analyses at the group level. On the other hand, we needed a universe in which "influences" on the individual decision-maker and the decision-making group could be studied in a relatively uniform context. In particular, we sought a universe which provided a basic environmental, political, and legal uniformity against which city-by-city differences could be appraised. We therefore decided on a single metropolitan region in a single state in which we could assume certain constants to be present—such as *relative* economic growth, similar institutional arrangements and political patterns, identical state statutory requirements, and so on.

The price paid for this research design should be obvious. The San Francisco Bay metropolitan region is quite unlike any other metropolitan region, including even the Los Angeles metropolitan area, and it differs significantly from the Chicago, Boston, or New York metropolitan complexes. Undoubtedly, metropolitan regions, despite internal differences, can be compared as ecological units in their own right. But as our units of analysis are individual or collective decision-makers in the cities of a particular, and in many respects internally unique region, the parameters imposed on our data by the choice of the San Francisco Bay metropolitan area recommend the greatest caution in extending, whether by analogy or inference, our findings to councils or councilmen in other metropolitan regions of other states.

All of this is not to say that particular analyses enlightened by theoretical concerns of a general nature cannot be absorbed into the growing body of political science knowledge. The City Council Research Project consciously built on previous research in other settings, seeking to identify and measure influences that have an impact on legislative processes and legislative products. The effect of the role orientations of councilmen with regard to their constituents, interest groups, or administrative officials may be compared with the effect of parallel orientations in larger legislative bodies. Their socialization and recruitment experiences, their differing styles of representational behavior, or their political strategies are probably influences not unlike those found elsewhere. Similarly, the relationships among individuals in a small group and the norms guiding their conduct may be compared with equivalent patterns in larger legislative bodies. Perceptions of the wider metropolitan environment and its problems, on one hand, and of the city environment and its problems, on the other hand, and how these perceptions affect council behavior and outputs are of general theoretical interest. In terms of the developing theory of legislative behavior and processes, therefore, the data collected by the Project and utilized in the monographs of this series have an import that transcends the boundaries of the particular metropolitan region in which they were collected.

The Research Context

San Francisco and its neighboring eight counties have experienced an extraordinary population growth rate since the end of World War II. Many of the wartime production workers and military personnel who traveled to or through this region decided to settle here permanently in the postwar years; they and thousands of others were attracted by moderate climate year around, several outstanding universities, closeness to the Pacific Ocean and its related harbors, headquarters for hundreds of West Coast branches of national firms and, of course, the delightful charm of San Francisco itself. Other resources and assets exist in abundance: inviting ski resorts and redwood parks are within short driving distance; hundreds of miles of ocean lie to the immediate west; mile after mile of grape vineyards landscape the nearby Livermore and Napa valleys. All of these, linked by the vast San Francisco Bay and its famous bridges, make this one of the nation's most distinctive and popular metropolitan regions.

Larger than the state of Connecticut and almost as large as New Jersey and Massachusetts combined, this nine-county region now houses four million people; about six million more are expected by 1980. At the time of the study, ninety cities and at least five hundred special districts served its residents.

As has been pointed out already, no claim can be made that the San Francisco Bay region is typical of other metropolitan areas; indeed, it differs considerably on a number of indicators. Unlike most of the other sizable metropolitan regions, the Bay region has experienced its major sustained population boom in the 1950's and 1960's. This metropolitan area is also atypical in that it has not one major central city but three—namely San Francisco, Oakland, and San Jose. And while San Francisco continues to be the "hub" and the region's dominant city, Oakland and San Jose are rival economic and civic centers. San Jose, moreover, anticipates that its population will triple to nearly a million people in the next twenty years. Of additional interest is the fact that this region has pioneered in the creation of one of the nation's prototypes of federated urban governmental structures. Its Association of Bay Area Governments, organized in 1961, has won national attention as one of the first metropolitan councils of local governments.

Although in many respects unlike other metropolitan regions, the San Francisco Bay region resembles some in the great diversity among its cities. Omitting San Francisco proper, 1965 city populations ranged from 310 to 385,700. Population densities in 1965 ranged from 71 to 12,262 persons per square mile. The rate of population growth between 1960 and 1965 ranged from zero to 204 percent. Median family incomes ranged from $3,582 to $23,300, and percent nonwhite from 0.1 to 26.4.

Institutionally, the governments of the cities in the San Francisco Bay region are predominantly of the council-manager or council-administrator form, although some of the very small cities may rely on the chief engineer rather than on a manager or administrator. Cities may be either of the "charter" or "general law" type. Charter cities differ from general law cities in having greater control over election laws, the size of their councils, the pay of municipal officers, and tax rate limitations. General law cities have five councilmen, while charter cities may have more than this number. Among the cities included in the research, the number of councilmen per city ranged from five to thirteen.

All local officials in California, including, of course, those interviewed in the City Council Research Project, are elected under a nonpartisan system. With a few exceptions, councilmen run at large and against the entire field of candidates. In five cities there is a modified district election plan in which candidates stand in a particular district but all voters cast ballots for any candidate. Ten cities elect the mayor separately; in the remaining cities the mayor is either the candidate receiving the highest number of votes or is selected by vote of the council.

Council candidates must have been residents of the community

Map E–1
Bay Area Place Names

for at least one year prior to their election. For the most part they are elected to serve two-year terms, though charter cities may vary this. Only three cities have tenure limitations. The great majority of councilmen receive no compensation for their services or, if any, only a token compensation to cover expenses. For most, the council is a part-time activity.

The powers of the city councilmen may be exercised only as a group; that is, individual councilmen have no power to act alone. The council may meet only at duly convened public meetings and at a place designated by ordinance. Council meetings must be regularly scheduled and held no less than once a month, but when council action is required between regularly scheduled meetings, the statutes allow procedures for calling special meetings. The "Brown Act," passed in 1953 and in effect during the time our interviewing took place, requires all council meetings to be public and publicized, except for executive sessions on personnel matters.

The Data Bases

Five sets of data were generated or systematized by the Project. First, data from the U.S. Census of Population for 1960 and estimates for 1965 served a variety of analytical purposes. Because the data included in the census and its categories are well known, we need not say more about this data set. Specific uses made of census data and the rationale for such uses are explained in each monograph wherever appropriate. All members of the research team were involved in readying the census data for analysis.

Second, data concerning city income, resources, and expenditures were available in the State Controller's *Annual Report of Financial Transactions Concerning Cities of California.* These reports include breakdowns which are suitable for comparative analysis of Bay region cities for the year 1958–1959 through 1965–1966. How the measures derived from this data set were handled is described in appropriate places of the monograph series where the data are used. Robert Eyestone was largely responsible for preparing this data set.

Third, local election data over a ten-year period, 1956 through 1966, were collected by Gordon Black, with the collaboration of Willis D. Hawley at the Institute of Governmental Studies, University of California, Berkeley. These data were obtained directly from the various cities, and they include the voting returns for each of five elections in each city, the registration figures for the city at each election period, and a variety of facts about individual candidates. These facts include incumbency, partisan affiliation, length of time in office, and the manner in which the incumbents gained office, whether by appointment or by election. A number of measures were constructed from these data, including measures of competition, partisan composition, voluntary retirement, forced turnover, and so forth. Descriptions of these measures can be found in the monographs which employ them.

Fourth and fifth, the core of the data on which the analyses are based come from interviews with city councilmen or from self-administered questionnaires filled out by councilmen. These two data sets need more detailed exposition.

1. Interview data

With the exception of a city incorporated while the field work was under way (Yountville) and the city of San Francisco itself, interviews were sought with 488 city councilmen holding office in all the other eighty-nine cities of the San Francisco Bay area. Although interviews were held with some members of the board of supervisors of the city-county of San Francisco, these interviews are not used in this and the other monographs owing to the city's unique governmental structure and the highly professionalized nature of its legislative body.

In two of the eighty-nine cities (Millbrae and Emeryville), all councilmen refused to be interviewed. In the remaining eighty-seven cities, 435 incumbent councilmen were interviewed. This constitutes 89 percent of the total population or 91 percent of the councilmen from the eighty-seven cities which cooperated in the study. The interviews were conducted by members of the research team or by professional interviewers. Most of the respondents were interviewed in their homes, places of business, or city hall offices. All of them had been invited to visit the Stanford campus, and a small number accepted the invitation and were interviewed there.

Although the bulk of the interviewing was done between January and April 1966, some councilmen were interviewed as late as June 1967. The interview schedule was an extensive one. It included some 165 major open-end questions and additional probes, ranging over a wide variety of topics. Every effort was made to record verbatim the comments which most councilmen supplied in abundance. The interviews lasted from two to five hours or longer and averaged about three hours. Parts of the interview schedule were pretested as early as 1962 and as late as 1965, with councilmen in the metropolitan region itself and with councilmen in a neighboring county.

The interview data were coded by members of the research team responsible for particular analyses. The coded data were recorded on seventeen machine readable storage cards. They will be made available for secondary analysis on tape in due time, upon completion of all studies in *The Urban Governors* series.

2. *Questionnaire*

In addition to the interview, each respondent was asked to fill out a questionnaire made up of closed questions. These included a set of thirty-five check-list items, two pages of biographical items, and a set of fifty-eight agree-disagree attitude items. The strategy of self-administered questionnaires was dictated by the length of the interview, for, in spite of its length, the data needs of the team members could not be satisfied by the interview instrument alone. The questionnaires were left with each respondent by the interviewer. If at all possible, interviewers were instructed to have the questionnaires filled out by the respondent immediately upon completion of the interview, but the length of the interview often did not permit this, and respondents were then asked to return the questionnaires by mail. As a result, there was some loss of potential data because councilmen neglected to return the completed forms. Nevertheless, of the 435 councilmen who were interviewed, 365, or 84 percent, completed the questionnaires. Perhaps the greatest strategic mistake in this procedure was our failure to administer the biographical and demographic background items as part of the interview.

The Sample: A Brief Profile

Although individual demographic data for all 435 councilmen who were interviewed are not available, our sample of 365 for which the data are at hand is probably representative. We shall present, therefore, a brief profile of these respondents.

On the average, San Francisco Bay region councilmen are well educated and have comfortable incomes (see Figure E–1). They are engaged in either business or professional activities. Table E–1 shows the principal lines of work of those council members who are not retired or housewives.

Councilmen in the Bay region are predominantly middle-aged, usually coming to the council while in their forties or around fifty years of age. The turnover rate of city councilman positions is relatively high, with only a few members staying in office for more than three or four terms. The data in Figure E–1 show that close to 70 percent of the councilmen came into office for the first time within the previous five years. In open-end conversations with councilmen, many responded that they looked upon the job as

Table E–1
Principal Employment of City Councilmen
(of Employed Councilmen) (N = 351)

Manufacturing, Utilities	22%
Banking, Insurance, Accountancy	21
Business, Commerce, Real Estate	13
Lawyer	10
Construction, Trucking	16
Civil Servant, Public Administration	14
Agriculture	4
	100%

Figure E-1

Background Profile of San Francisco Bay Region City Councilmen

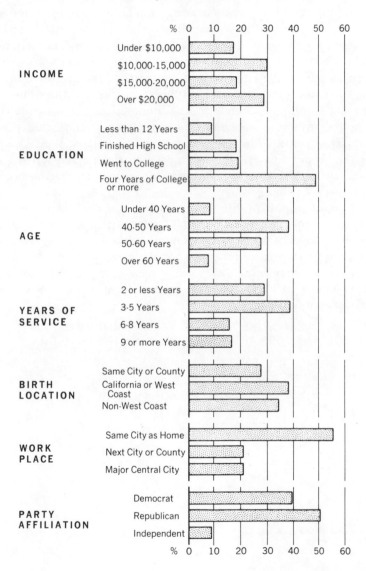

a community service, as something that should be rotated among the local activists like themselves.

Fifty-six percent of the Bay region councilmen who are currently employed work in their home community, the community on whose city council they serve. This is not too surprising, for it is customary for local "home town" businessmen and lawyers to be involved in community service and civic undertakings, which often constitute the cheif recruitment vehicle for the identification of city political leadership. While a majority of the councilmen are employed in their local communities, it is instructive to note that most of the councilmen are not natives of their present city or county. Most, however, are California or West Coast natives. Approximately a third moved to the Bay region from other parts of the United States, with about a dozen having been born in some other country.

The background profile data also indicate that Republicans outnumber the Democrats by an 11 percent margin in the Bay region's nonpartisan city council posts, although during recent years the party registration rates for the general electorate have favored the Democratic party in approximately a three-to-two ratio. Nine percent of the councilmen identify themselves as Independents.

Index